EVERY NEW BROOM SWEEPS CLEAN

An authorized biography of

Harold E. Bailey

by

W. J. Drescher

ISBN 0-9709421-0-9

51500

9 780970 942104

EVERY NEW BROOM SWEEPS CLEAN

W. J. Drescher
Copyright 2001

Printed in the United States
ISBN: 0-9709421-0-9

Published and Printed by:
CITY PRINTING COMPANY
36 West Wood St. • Youngstown, OH 44503

To order more copies
of this book contact:

W. J. Drescher
P.O. Box 400
Leavittsburg, Ohio
44430

1-877-998-8170

SPECIAL THANKS TO:

I wish to give thanks to all those friends and relatives who listened to my incessant ramblings while I wrote this story. I hope they aren't totally hypnotized by my continuous talking.

To Ken Brayer, words cannot repay your help. You helped me travel down my first path to actually having my book published.

I especially thank the Friendly Trapper for giving me the opportunity to tell his story. I love you, Trap.

CONTENTS

INTRODUCTION

After hearing only a small part of the Friendly Trapper's life story, I marvel that he has risen above so many major tragedies, obstacles and disappointments to get to the prominent position he holds today. He has appeared on more than one television show and currently appears on WKBN network. He also performs on multiple radio broadcasts sharing his secrets to a healthy environment free from pests.

I wanted to immortalize this man's history for future generations to enjoy but I didn't have the courage to ask him. Then, a golden opportunity came to me and it was mine to grasp or ignore.

Ron Verb, a favorite talk-show host with WKBN radio, casually mentioned that he was broadcasting from the parking lot of the Blast From the Past Restaurant in Boardman. And to give credibility to the great food, he announced that the Friendly Trapper was having dinner inside.

I had heard Harold E. Bailey or as he is fondly called, the Friendly Trapper, numerous times on the radio. I had watched him on television. I had purchased his book to give as gifts to special people, myself being included as one of those special people. And I had always wanted to meet him from the day I first heard his infectious laughter bubbling over the airways.

I walked into the restaurant confident that I would recognize him anywhere. Surely, he would have an entourage of people around him and I would have to fight my way through the crowd to talk to him. But I couldn't find him. No one was wearing the white floppy hat with the blue hatband that has become his trademark.

The man pointed out to me was sitting alone in a booth by the window. It was obvious from his dress that he had been helping someone with a 'critter' problem. The white t-shirt he was wearing sported an assortment of painted bugs on the front. The dark blue gabardine 'work' pants were wrinkled and had a few smudges of mud around the hemline. This medium-sized man's face showed no signs of the rough, leathery skin so many acquire from spending years outside in the hot sun of summer and the bone-chilling cold of winter.

I approached him not really knowing what I was going to say or even if I would be welcomed. After all, I was a total stranger who was rudely interrupting his quiet dinner. He looked up at me as I stood beside the booth and a large smile came upon his face. He actually seemed surprised that I would recognize him. He was genuinely pleased that I had taken the opportunity to say hello and invited me to join him. I knew then and there that fame had not changed this midwestern man. The Friendly Trapper considers himself just a common, ordinary man from Canfield, Ohio.

I liked him immediately! My intended five-minute conversation stretched into forty at the blink of an eye. He had so much to say and I was enthralled with all that he was saying.

Trapper's dinner was served at some point during our conversation. The waitress apologized, "Mr. Bailey. I'm afraid that your dinner may be a little too cold for you. Would you want me to have the cook put it in the microwave oven for a minute or two?"

"No. That's not necessary. It'll be fine just the way it is," he assured her.

The plate held a meal that seemed a bit odd for such a prominent man. But I should have known better. What else would a common, ordinary man from Canfield, Ohio enjoy more? Meat loaf and mashed potatoes dripping with gravy and a side order of fresh kernel corn suddenly seemed very appropriate.

Out of the blue, he asked, "Who sent you to me?"

I assured him, "I just happened to hear on the radio that you were here."

He again asked who had sent me and I repeated what I had said.

"No. Somebody sent you to me," Trapper said with his finger pointed skyward referring to God. "You are going to write my story. I'm a good judge of people and I know you're a good person."

I was totally shocked that this man had made that statement. I had never mentioned that I am an author, not even once during our conversation. I am honored that he has chosen me for the job.

CHAPTER ONE

GETTING STARTED

The Friendly Trapper slid out of the bronze Grand Marquis effortlessly. I watched him walk briskly toward the restaurant door. There were no obvious signs of his age. He stood straight and tall. I saw no telltale limps or hesitations in his walk that one usually associates with an older person's arthritis. I saw none of the droopy ill-fitting clothing commonly seen on an old man. Yet, I knew he no longer had the darker colored hair of a young man.

Harold E. Bailey hadn't noticed me sitting in a booth awaiting his arrival at the McDonald's Restaurant in Canfield, Ohio. He and his constant companion, Marie Dornshuld, approached the serving counter for an order of steaming coffee and warm blueberry muffins.

Some of the people behind the counter recognized him immediately. He was wearing the soft floppy white hat with a blue hatband, his trademark, perched atop his head. Others standing in front of the counter turned when they heard his infectious chuckle. Their faces changed from having that "staring at nothing in particular look" to faces plastered with smiles. They turned his way even though he wasn't directing his conversation towards them.

This restaurant was obviously a community-gathering place. Almost instantly, people began walking up to Trapper to bid their friend a good morning. He knew them by name and asked about their wives, their children, and their jobs.

Others who weren't known to Trapper approached him, too. They felt comfortable talking to this friendly man and he greeted them as if he'd known them all his life.

Marie had stepped a short distance behind his back and away from him. She seemed barely noticeable as she stood in front of the four-foot high counter that held the straws and napkins. It was almost as if she liked to blend in with the background scenery allowing Trapper to receive all the attention.

Her silvery white hair was combed away from her small face and there was a gentle smile on her thin, rose-colored lips as she watched Trapper interacting with the crowd. She wore a pale gold jacket with the words "The Friendly Trapper" embroidered on its back. There was no doubt that she was waiting for the man who had suddenly become the center of attraction at the McDonald's Restaurant. And there was no doubt that she was very proud of 'her man'.

I wondered if Trapper would remember what I looked like as I watched patiently from the mauve colored booth closest to the door. After all, we had only seen each other once for a short forty minutes. And it had been over a month since I barged into the Blast from the Past Restaurant to interrupt his dinner. To my amazement, he turned and smiled an acknowledging smile. As soon as he was able, he approached my booth and apologized for not coming over sooner.

"Let's go downstairs into the community room for the taping, OK?" he asked. "That way we won't be interrupted."

The stairs were very steep and the stairwell was narrow. The walls were covered with dark brown, almost black, paneling. It lent an eerie aura to the venture that would momentarily begin. But Trapper's sure footing never missed a step and he led me with confidence to the room built in the basement of the McDonald's Restaurant in Canfield, Ohio.

We entered a fairly large and dimly lit room. The dark paneling had been continued around the bottom half of the walls. The upper half was covered in dark gold wallpaper.

Trapper apparently had an unspoken authority in this restaurant. A McDonald's employee was seated at a table taking what appeared to be a well-deserved break. Trapper calmly took charge of our situation.

He asked her, "Would you mind taking your break in another part of the restaurant? We're having a meeting here and we'd like to meet in private."

She agreed without any hesitation then gathered her

newspaper and went upstairs.

Trapper sat comfortably on a padded chair across the table from Marie and I. Large fragrant cups of coffee were placed strategically on the table in front of us. "Wetting our whistle" was definitely a possibility since the audiotaping could take quite a long time. Our jackets hung over the backs of our chairs in case an unexpected cold draft threatened to disturb our comfort. We were prepared for the first all morning taping session of his memoirs.

His take-charge personality bled into our taping session as well. It was perfectly clear to both of us that he would assume the role of the expert and I would be the rookie who needed help. He showed me exactly what he thought needed done during the session. He told me exactly what he expected to happen as I pulled my inexpensive Sony tape recorder from its gray flannel pouch.

He then confidently attached the microphone to the neckband of his white T-shirt. The assortment of painted bugs on the front of the shirt peered at me from across the table. He happened to wear the same shirt as when I had first met him. He indicated that it was time to begin.

And we began. We started at Trapper's beginning.

CHAPTER TWO

FROM THE BEGINNING

George stood at the nursery window of Northside Hospital proudly watching the small infant sleeping in the bassinette. It was almost unbelievable that he and his wife, Laura, were so blessed on that day, April 21, 1928. Though he could only see his son's pink wrinkly face and hands, he fell in love with him instantly. He smiled as Harold Edward awoke and began crying for attention. It was feeding time and George knew his son wanted to be taken to his mother. George wished he could be present in Laura's hospital room as his son was given nourishment but that was forbidden by the hospital. Someone, even a child's father, might inadvertently bring an unwanted germ to the newborn.

Laura cooed motherly sounds to her son as he was placed in her arms by the nurse, "Oh, my beautiful son. You are so perfect. Um-m, you smell so good. Mama loves you so much."

She lovingly caressed his fuzzy head and his velvety arms. She felt elated that he could grasp her finger in his small hand. She thought how tiny he looked as he lay there with his legs curled close to his body. It seemed to Laura as if he'd always been a part of their family.

A week later, the big day had arrived. It was time to take Harold home to the house that was encircled with daffodils and tulips.

Harold wailed against the coldness of the hospital room as Laura removed his hospital gown. To soothe him, she sang softly as she dressed her son. He quieted immediately when he heard her singing. She finished dressing him by swaddling him in a hand crocheted blanket made specifically for this happy day.

Home for the Baileys was a house built by George and his brother Jim at 3223 Sheridan Rd. The tan sided house still stands in an area known to Youngstowners as Brownlee Woods. As was typical in those days, the cellar walls were erected using glazed blocks. The two-story home, dwarfed by a larger house just north of it, was considered small by today's standards. However, the dining room, the central gathering place for friends and family, was large enough to hold an oak table that would seat 15 people for dinner quite comfortably.

George and Laura considered their two-bedroom home to be of ample size to hold one other child. Harold's sister Audrey was born a few years later. The two children were the only children the Baileys would have.

The young children always managed to find something with which to play although toys were scarce. One game that they loved to play was "chase the tail". A part of the game was the pipeless furnace that heated the Bailey's home. Since there were no pipes to guide the heated air from one level to the next, holes were cut in the floors measuring approximately 12 inches by 12 inches. Metal register covers were placed over the holes to allow the air to rise but to prevent anyone from accidentally falling through to the lower level.

Real rabbit tails were the other part of the game. Audrey and Harold were given the rabbits' tails after George skinned the animals for meat. The children would lay the lighter-than-air balls on top of the register and wait impatiently. When the heated air rose upwards, the fluffy tails would float towards the ceiling. Audrey and Harold would giggle and run around the room trying to be the first one to catch the tails as they floated down towards the floor. It was a great game and one that was played often.

CHAPTER THREE

EARLY CHILDHOOD

Harold started first grade at Jackson Elementary School when he was 6 years old. He says the school was great and "all the students were lucky even though we walked to school."

One of the reasons that Harold considered the students to be lucky was that a central furnace, a definite luxury in the early depression days, heated the entire building. It wasn't necessary to have the pot-bellied coal stove in each classroom that was prominent in most schools.   These lucky students' daily duties didn't include shoveling coal into a black metal monster waiting to burn anyone who came near.

Other luxuries for the students at Jackson Elementary were indoor plumbing and bathroom facilities. Anyone having the pleasure, or perhaps the not so nice pleasure, of visiting an outhouse can attest to the fact that indoor plumbing was indeed a luxury, especially when you were a small child. When 'nature called', a small trek down the hallway was much preferable to a long walk outdoors. And midwestern winter snows could prove to be a time-consuming obstacle when making a mad dash for the outhouse. Putting on coats, boots, and other protective clothing when you're in a hurry can make getting there in time almost next to impossible. And when you're 6 years old, nature might shout out loudly every hour or two.

Elementary school teachers including Miss Davis and Miss Weddick tried to give Harold the best education that they could. They encouraged the wiggly child to pay more attention but he continually shuffled his feet under his desk or tapped his pencil on his desk. They nudged him toward the right direction but he just couldn't get there as fast as the teachers had hoped.

"It took me a long time to get from 1st to 2nd to 3rd grade," Harold professes. "I was indeed a challenging student."

One can only imagine what it was like for Harold. The young boy had so many thoughts passing through his mind at one time that it seemed like a gigantic river of words flowed through his brain each and every second. Everything else in the room added to the turmoil in his mind and disturbed his concentration. The other children quietly turning their book pages, the soft creaking of the wooden floors, the persistent ticking of the clock, and noises not even noticed by the other children intruded into his thoughts. It would soon become impossible to keep that rush of words under his control and an even greater impossibility to ignore the commotions outside his body. Harold would either need to talk, to move, or to give up on whatever he was doing. It was difficult for teachers to understand that it simply wasn't his choice to ignore all the sounds and he would be punished regularly.

But he couldn't control the hoards of thoughts passing through his mind no matter how hard he tried. And it was intensely difficult to concentrate on only one thought at a time.

For Harold, school was as confining as prison walls. Not that he didn't enjoy the teachers and the other students. He did. He always liked to be around them. He just didn't want to be within the confines of a building that brought him so much trouble.

Harold would always try to be the first one to run through the school's door to the freedom and the fresh smells of the outdoors when the bell rang for dismissal. He'd rush from the building pretending that he didn't have to return the next day. He had more important things to do than to study his schoolbooks. He was tired of listening to lectures that most of the time only added more turmoil to the already overflowing river in his mind.

In the winter, Harold loved to go sled riding, "Hey, everyone. Let's head to the hill. The snow's packing good and my sled is all set."

All the neighborhood children headed for their favorite spot and Power's Way was that special place. It was known by all the children around Brownlee Woods that this was the steepest, fastest hill in all of Youngstown.

Harold prepared for days ahead of time. He licked his lips in anticipation while plying layer after layer of paraffin on his rusty sled runners. He wanted his sled to be the fastest one to race down the hill.

The children would all line up at the top of the hill, run as fast as they could then flop onto their bellies on top of their sleds. They steered their sleds from side to side hoping not to tip over as they steered clear of each other's sleds. Sometimes they gave each other rides by doubling up on the sleds, one child lying on top of the other's back. Dragging their feet was the only way to stop at the bottom of the hill even though it did force snow into their boots.

There were numerous races every day. They squealed and shouted cheers to each other through chattering teeth in-between the uncontrollable shivering of their cold, excited bodies. The neighborhood champion was the one who had ridden the farthest or went the fastest down the hill. They would even declare who was the bravest by measuring who had taken the most chances.

The children had so much fun that time slipped by without them knowing. They would become freezing cold a lot faster than they realized, too. Their gloves, socks, jackets and pants became soaked; dripping wet with melted snow. They ignored the sloshing sounds of their wet feet moving inside their boots. Their fingers and toes became numb but they still wouldn't want to quit.

Running up the hill, dragging their sleds behind them, the Brownlee Wood's neighborhood kids never acknowledged to themselves or to each other how tired they had become. They had to take just one more ride down the ice-covered hill before going home.

The final decision to end the day's fun was always too late to save any of the much-needed energy to trudge home. The long slow laborious walk caused pain with each step. Their feet and toes throbbed. Their fingers would be stinging; the children having no way to keep their hands warm inside wet dripping gloves. The walk would seem endless with the extra weight of their heavy, water-laden clothes.

But no matter how painful their feet and hands became or how cold they were or how endless their walk home seemed, they couldn't wait to come back the next time for more sled riding on Power's Way hill. To Harold and his friends, this was the best sled-riding hill in the entire world. They were absolutely sure of it.

Summer was a time of total freedom for Harold. He didn't have to attend school and he was happy whether he was working with his father or doing chores or fishing in a lake.

However, he loved fishing more than anything else. Carrying his favorite fishing pole in one hand and a bucket of fat wiggly night crawlers in the other, he'd walk through leg-cutting weeds to get to Hamilton Lake, which was approximately 10-15 miles from home. He'd spend as much time as he could on a sunny summer day sitting beside the lake, passing away the time as some might say just drowning worms.

Harold would sit and wait for hours if necessary for the first signs of fish swimming in the water. He'd watch for tiny circles forming on the surface of the lake indicating that a school of fish lay in wait under the muddy water. He'd become mesmerized by the blue sky and the billowy clouds passing by that were reflected in the water. Staring into the water, waiting for a fish to tug on his line was ever peaceful for him.

Harold especially enjoyed the lake when the moon was bright and it was time for the suckers to spawn. He'd look for the spawning fish gathered in shallow water by watching for ripples on the water's surface. When he saw the ripples, he'd know there would be a circular nest built on the lake's bottom that was made out of stones. If fish had picked white lucky stones to be included in the nest, the nest would appear to glow in the dark.

Harold took a Hensley fork with him when the fish were spawning instead of the usual fishing pole and bucket of worms. Harold described a Hensley fork by saying that "it has lots of teeth in it." He would catch the fish by scooping them onto the fork and tossing them onto the bank. After reaching his quota of fish for the night, he'd pick up the squirming catch, shove them into a sack, and take them home for the family to eat for dinner.

Annoyances associated with fishing went unnoticed by Harold. The fishy smell rising from the water didn't bother him. And if it happened to be a day when the mosquitoes were especially fierce or the bugs swarmed around his sweaty head, he didn't mind that either. He was doing the one thing he loved most in the summer.

When Harold was six years old he developed rheumatic fever, a serious disease that usually follows a case of strep throat. The doctor told the family that he had probably caught the disease from wearing leaky boots. Harold's illness lasted for six months. For six weeks, he was bedridden and not permitted to go downstairs. He had a high fever and pain and swelling around his joints. His leg jerked up and down constantly and wouldn't stop no matter how hard Harold tried to control it.

The only other thing Harold recalls about the illness was his mother running up and down the steps leading to his bedroom. She would bring him ice cream or anything else he requested. He remembers that Laura lost a lot of weight that he attributes to her worrying about her son and because she seemed to be constantly in motion.

After being made to stay in bed for that long, Harold started to closely pay attention to his health habits. He tried to stay out of the rain and the cold so he wouldn't become ill again.

A short while after he had recovered, he decided to go fishing again. He returned home momentarily because he wasn't feeling well. He was put to bed and Dr. W.W. Wile, the family physician, confirmed that once again he had rheumatic fever. The doctor advised George and Laura to wrap his legs in woolen cloths and that the bedroom's temperature should be kept hotter than normal. This time the illness left Harold with a permanently enlarged heart.

Harold says, "That enlarged heart kept me out of the service. But I never pay any attention to it. It doesn't slow me down and I eat everything that is put before me."

When he was a little older, about eight or nine years old, Harold found that if he stuck out his thumb while walking along the road, someone would recognize him and give him a ride. He'd hitchhike on the better days all the way to Lion's Blvd in Poland to fish in Hamilton Lake.

"That was always the best fishing spot. It was a quiet place to reflect on your thoughts. It was safe for young children to be there alone. And it's the only place I know to catch suckers alive," said Harold.

None of the fish or fish parts was ever wasted. The fish that the Baileys didn't eat were saved for Laura's rose garden. She would spade the dirt loosening the hard clay soil, which this northeastern Ohio area is known for, and bury the fish and the fish parts around the plants. Fish are hailed to be the best fertilizer for rose bushes and Harold declares that it surely must be true. His mother had some of the most beautiful roses in the entire neighborhood.

Laura took care of the home and the family. She would rise in the morning, get dressed, and cook breakfast for everyone before they left for the day. She prepared cornmeal mush as a hot cereal with milk one morning and fried cornmeal mush patties the next. If the family were lucky, a link of sausage would have been bought on grocery shopping day to be fried with the cornmeal mush. It wasn't a fancy breakfast but it helped stave off the hunger until noon and it wasn't too expensive.

George, as was typical in the days of the Great Depression, was the sole breadwinner of the family. He worked for the Blueflame Kerosene Company. His job was to drive a flatbed truck along a specified route both within and outside the city. He'd pick up the old-fashioned metal gasoline cans that people had set alongside the road. The cans were hauled back to the company, filled with either kerosene or gasoline, and returned to the customer's homes.

Sometimes Harold would be permitted to go to work with George. When he was allowed to go, Harold loved sitting beside his father on the leather seat, jostling up and down with every bump and hole that the truck hit in the road.

George only allowed him to accompany him once or twice in the wintertime no matter how many times Harold pleaded. The truck's heater wasn't powerful enough to keep both of them warm.

In the summer, however, it was a different story. Harold was permitted to join his father often. The summer heat could climb into the 80's and the only option to get relief from the heat was to allow air to gush in through the opened windows. An air conditioner was one of those luxuries that hardly anyone could afford to have in his/her vehicles.

When Harold would complain about the summer heat, George would tell his son, "If you want to stay cool, just roll the windows down."

Harold says he came to believe that it worked, too. He'd roll the window down and he really did feel much cooler.

To Harold, George was magnificent! He was gifted with what Harold considered a special talent. When George returned to his factory with the empty containers and couldn't remember whether he needed to fill the cans with kerosene or gasoline, he would remove the lids and smell some of the fumes that wafted out of the can. He would know with one quick whiff which fuel to pour into the container.

This talent was especially important because the fuels could not be used interchangeably. The customers used different fuels in their tractors and their stoves and other appliances. If the fuels were mistakenly put in the wrong engine, the motors were ruined thereby placing an additional financial burden upon those least able to pay for it and George would be held responsible.

Occasionally, George would find an old black inner tube to bring home to his children. They would scream with delight when they saw it because Harold and Audrey knew it was time to add another favorite toy to their collection, a modified slingshot.

George first cut a board to a length of ten inches to make the toy. He'd bring a clothespin and a nail along with the board to his workbench. Breaking the clothespin in half, he attached one half of it to the front of the board and one half to the back placing both on the topside of the board. He pounded the nail to the bottom side to serve as a handle. The 16-inch inner tube was wrapped around the clothespin halves and was stretched with their fingers as far as the rubber would expand. Harold and Audrey would then release the inner tube, allowing it to fly off the clothespins.

"If the tube had a lot of zip, it would fly fifteen or twenty feet when it was released. We would find old things to use for targets and see who could hit the most," Harold chuckles. They used cans, paper bags, spools, or stand up clothespins for their targets.

"I never remember my dad playing baseball with me though," Harold said softly and wistfully as if he almost didn't want to be heard. Then he raised the volume of his voice and continued, "He did have a double-barreled shotgun and that poor rabbit never had a chance."

On one particular Friday at sunup, Harold remembers his father waking him. "Harold, it's time to get up. It's time you learned to hunt."

They loaded their guns into their 1936 Chrysler. They also tucked a lunch that Laura had fixed for them into the automobile and headed to the woods for an all day hunting excursion. They wouldn't be returning home until after dusk.

Harold recalls that George always had Harold stand behind him while hunting. Harold still isn't sure if it was to protect him or to pick George up off the ground when he fired his double-barreled shotgun. He also thinks that possibly he was told to stand behind him so he could run for help if there was a problem.

They always took their favorite hunting dog, Belle, to assist with the hunt. Belle was a purebred beagle who had twenty-two inch long ears that hung down below her paws. Harold never quite figured out how she managed but he never saw her trip on them. And George had trained her to be a good 'rabbit dog'. If a rabbit was chased out of its hiding place and George missed shooting it with his shotgun, Harold and he would stand perfectly still. In a short time, Belle would chase the rabbit right back to where they were standing giving George a second chance to capture supper.

On one occasion, a hunting trip for Belle proved to be more than just a chance to chase after rabbits.

A 1936 Chrysler was manufactured with a rack attached to the back of the car because there was no space built inside its body for a trunk. The rack would fold out and down so that it resembled a wire table useful for carrying extra items. There was no room inside the Chrysler for Belle so George placed her in a box. The box was secured to the rack.

A concerned Harold said, "Dad, Belle will fly out of the box. I don't want her to get hurt."

"Nah she won't. Take a look. I tied it real tight and she's sitting quietly in the box."

Harold laughs, "We went over some railroad tracks, and poor Belle flew out. She didn't get hurt but she sure went aflyin'."

Because George was a good hunter, the Baileys always had plenty of frozen meat while others were scrounging for any that they could buy. George cleaned everything that he caught and the family rule was that they ate, sold or gave away everything that was caught.

Being careful not to drool on his shirt, Harold says, "Give me someone who knows how to fix that wild meat and some old-fashioned sweet potatoes, and sweet onion, and oh man... What a meal!"

Harold remembers his mother saying one day after looking at all the rabbits hanging up in the garage, "Geez George, we wish you'd catch something else. We're so tired of rabbit. We've had fried rabbit, stewed rabbit, rabbit pie and everything else."

In an attempt to appease Laura, George would catch something different but they wouldn't eat those animals. He'd catch possums, raccoons, and ground hogs and remove the animal's fur being careful to leave one foot untouched and attached to the carcass. He would then hang the skins to dry in the garage so that they could be sold for money to add to the family's coffers.

When there were enough carcasses, Harold and George would take them to the Monkey's nest, an area now called West Lakes Crossing. George would place a board from armrest to armrest in the car and they would lay the carcasses on the board. Families and WPA (Work Progress Administration) workers would come and purchase the animals. However, they would only buy the meat if the paw was visible. The people wanted to be absolutely positive what kind of animal they were buying.

George's job at Blueflame Kerosene came to an end. He then became employed as a watchman at the Vienna Airport located on State Rt. 193. The airport, called the Youngstown Regional Airport today, wasn't totally constructed. On a day that the runway was being built and the cement had been recently poured, George had taken Harold hunting in the woods surrounding the airport.

"Son, do you want to leave your mark in the world?"

Being a small boy, Harold looked up at his father and asked, "What does that mean?"

"It means that when you do something important and anyone sees it even years from now, they'd know that you were the one that did it."

"OK. That sounds great. But what should I do?"

George led him to the runway. While holding his hand so he wouldn't topple, George told Harold to gently place his foot in the fresh cement.

If anyone knew exactly where that footprint was made, Harold is positive it could still be seen today. And now everyone knows whose mark was left in the world at the Vienna Airport runway.

George's homestead and many of his relatives lived in Lordstown, Ohio. The Bailey homestead was only a few houses west and across the street from the church on Palmyra Road. Some of the relatives continue to reside in the home today.

Family outings to the small town were a particular highlight and gave the Bailey family a short respite from the details of their everyday routines. They would pile into the Chrysler and head for church services or to a family get-together.

The ministers of the Lordstown Lutheran church located on Palmyra Road at the end of South Leavitt Road have seen Baileys in the congregation for many years. The quaint white country church complete with a steeple at the roof's peak continues to beckon members of the Bailey family for Sunday services at Bailey's Corners.

Harold recalls when the church held its first night service. He distinctly remembers that in order to hold a service after dark, members had to choose the tallest man to care for the gas mantle lights. Elmer Harner, measuring well over six foot tall, was the only parishioner who could reach as high as the ceiling. He was placed in charge of taking down the gaslights, pumping the fuel reservoir with air, and, after relighting the mantles he would hang the lights on hooks near the ceiling.

In the winter when the family intended to go out and about in the car, George would put a granite soap-stone block on the living room register until it was warmed. He'd then wrap a blanket around the soapstone thus keeping it clean. The children could keep their feet warm in the backseat of the Chrysler by sitting with their feet on top of the block all the way to their destination. The soapstone was also heated if company came to the house and the guests needed some extra comforting after a trek in the cold.

Summer time found the Baileys traveling to Lordstown often for family picnics that included both George's and Laura's families. The adults would sit on lawn chairs and picnic tables catching up on the latest family gossip while the children played games in the nearby yard.

A hog roast, sometimes a part of the menu for the picnic, was always a special treat for Harold "because it was a family thing." The hogs were scalded and dressed and skewered onto a spit. They would be left to cook all day over an open fire that was stoked with logs by the men. The flame was kept continually at the same height so as not to undercook or burn the meat. When the meat got firm, the hog was "butchered and salted down." Some of the meat was eaten that day and the rest was saved for future dinners.

The saved meat would be stored in a small smoke house built by the family. A blend of hickory, apple, and cherry wood smoke would be allowed to penetrate the meat slowly over several days. The wood mixture turned the smoked pork into a mouth-watering delicacy.

Sausage links were also made on the hog-roasting day. Meat that had been ground and seasoned was shoved into the hog's natural casings, its intestines. Harold loved to shock people by telling them about the intestines. He loved to see the looks on their faces when they realized that the artificial casings used today weren't invented yet.

He elaborates, "Of course the intestines had to be washed numerous times both inside and out before it was used. But somehow I forgot to mention that fact until people have had time to think about what the hog's natural casings were."

He continued, "When we Baileys treated ourselves to a big sit-down breakfast, we children knew we were having eggs, pancakes and homemade sausage. Um-m, um-m. It was the most mouth-watering sausage in the land. And I never dirtied my mouth for just one egg. I'd always have to have two or three."

Chickens roamed freely in the Lordstown families' yards so they could scrounge for food wherever they found it. Their favorite food was kernels of dried corn that they had pecked off corncobs laying on the ground.

A fun game for the children was played after they gathered the empty dried corncobs. Placing a large chicken feather in each end, they would toss the corncobs up towards the sky. If the children had chosen corncobs that were light enough and feathers that were big enough, the corncobs floated to earth in a twirling motion. The children had homemade helicopters and races were run as part of the day's happenings.

CHAPTER FOUR

A HAPPY CHILDHOOD IS TAKEN AWAY

Aunt Bonnie tenderly placed Harold's smaller hand in hers. Walking slowly and quietly, she led him to the bathroom. She had never acted this way before and the knot in his stomach told him that he should follow her without making a sound.

Harold looked up into her eyes. He couldn't understand what was happening. He could see that Aunt Bonnie knew something that he didn't. He knew that whatever the secret was, it was something very wrong.

They stood in front of the bathroom sink. She dipped a washcloth into the running warm water. Wringing the excess water from out of the cloth, she began running the washcloth ever so softly across his cheeks and forehead and chin. Why would his aunt look so sad when she was just washing his face?

He stared at her face as her lips parted to speak. He knew she would begin telling him what she had brought him here to say. But he also knew he didn't want to hear whatever it was going to be. He should run away before his ears could hear the first sounds.

But he had to stay. His wobbly legs wouldn't allow him to move without collapsing to the floor. And he could hear people crying.

"Harold, your father has passed away. Your father died from what we call a stroke. He is now in Heaven with God and the rest of our family."

'That's impossible' thought Harold. 'He was just in the next room. Dad was in bed sleeping. The thin wall was the only thing separating him from them. But he couldn't have gone anywhere. I would have heard him shut the door or Mom would have told us.'

" Harold, you're the only man in your family now. You have to be strong for your mother and your sister. Your father would have wanted it that way."

'Maybe dad will just wake up and then everything will be all right. He can't leave us now. I'm too young to take care of Mom and Audrey. I don't know how. I'll just go yell at him and tell him to get up. Maybe if I shake him real hard he'll get out of bed and go downstairs to breakfast like he always does.'

"It's better for your father this way. He didn't feel a thing and he didn't suffer. But he never could have gotten better. And you know your father would never want to live if he couldn't do all the things he liked to do."

Harold guessed he could agree with Aunt Bonnie. 'It would have been terrible if Dad had suffered a stroke while driving his gasoline truck especially if the cans had been full. He might have wrecked the truck.

Someone might have hit him. Both incidents could have caused his truck to explode. Yes, it was better that Dad had passed away quietly in his bed.' No matter how terrible he felt, Harold was grateful that his father had died in their home.

His dad always said, "Every new broom sweeps clean." He knew his life was changed but he didn't know how.

CHAPTER FIVE

THE PATH TO ADULTHOOD

After George's death, life for the Baileys became extremely difficult. Laura had never worked outside the family home and she had no skills to get a good paying job. She couldn't drive and she didn't have enough money to own a car even if she could. But she was determined to raise her family in the home George had built. She would find a way to make money to pay the bills. She knew there had to be a way to keep the children clothed and fed.

Laura was an excellent cook so she decided that she would make bread and sell it. She told friends and relatives that she would be willing to bake for outside people. Would they please help her by telling others about it? Soon people began coming to the house to buy her delicious bread piping hot and fresh from the oven. Selling bread didn't bring in bundles of money but it did help with paying the bills.

Laura knew she still needed additional money so she used another skill at which she had become quite adept. All these years that she had been a wife and mother she had washed mountains of clothes for her family. So she began washing clothes for other people.

It didn't take long for Laura to become exhausted. She was trying diligently to use each and every waking hour efficiently. If she only had more time to bake more bread, wash more clothes, take care of her house and raise her two young children. Her mind had become dull with weariness.

She made a mistake that almost cost her dearly. She was washing clothes in her old but dependable electric wringer washer. She stood in front of the washer mechanically feeding clothes into the wringer, her mind wandering elsewhere. Sudden excruciating pain brought her mind back to reality in a hurry. Her right hand and arm had followed the clothes into the rollers of the wringer and they had become caught. Even though she was in agony, she somehow managed to reach the release button with her other hand. She was able to loosen the roller's tension that was squeezing her right arm so tightly.

For a few weeks she was unable to use her arm and hand therefore she was unable to earn some of the money she had come to depend. There were no sick benefits on this job and no worker's compensation. Laura couldn't bake until she could knead the dough. Laura, however, could still wash clothes with one hand.

Oftentimes, Laura would sing while she was doing the household chores. The children loved to listen to her and thought she had the voice of an angel. She would sing all the old favorite hymns that she sang at the Third Reform Church in Brownlee Woods; the church to which she would walk Harold and Audrey every Sunday for church services. People said you could hear her melodic soprano voice two blocks away and above all the rest of the choir members.

There was hardly ever enough money for store-bought clothes. Laura made most everything the family wore. In the evenings, the children watched their mother hand sewing their clothes. She used material from flour sacks or from old clothes that the children had outgrown. Every stitch she sewed was the exact same length on every piece of clothing. She tediously made sure of it.

Once, Laura saved enough money to buy Harold a pair of Knickers. She was so proud of how handsome and stylish her son looked in them. But Harold didn't care for them. Every Sunday, he'd have to wear those noisy pants.

He complained to his mother, "Mama, these pants are too noisy. All I hear is swish, swish, swish. They aren't even practical. I can't even wear them hunting. The noise chases all the animals too far ahead of us. Just ask Dave. He'll tell you."

Dave Claypool, a good friend of the family, took a liking to Harold and the feeling was mutual. He was kind to Harold and helped him whenever he could. Dave decided he would take Harold deer hunting. Dave bought Harold's hunting license and they drove in Dave's Pontiac to Cain Mountain in Pennsylvania. They stayed in a hunting cabin for the night.

To impress Dave, Harold had decided to wear those Knickers. He thought if his mom thought he was stylish in them maybe Dave would, too. But Dave hadn't noticed the pants until after they were already in the woods. Dave heard Harold's Knickers swishing behind him and the noise was echoing throughout the woods.

Dave turned and said, "What the heck's making so much noise?"

"My new Knickers. I wanted to look nice because I was going with you."

"Well, stand on that stump over there. You're scaring the rabbits away," said Dave.

"I'll let my two dogs chase the rabbits towards you. When you see one, shoot it."

What Dave didn't know was that a half-inch of ice had formed on the top of the wet stump he had pointed out to Harold. Eventually, the rabbit did come running towards Harold. Harold shot his trusty 12-gauge shotgun. The force of the gun's recoiling action knocked Harold off the stump. He landed flat on his back on the ground.

Harold lay there laughing and laughing even though the rabbit ran away. "There was no rabbit for dinner that night!"

The next day, the lady at the camp packed the men a lunch to put in their hunting coats. When they entered the woods, Harold says, "I wasn't paying attention where I was supposed to go 'cause I was eating that egg sandwich. I came to a Y in the path and I was supposed to turn right and stand there for a while. The guys were going to drive deer to me so I could get my first deer."

Instead, Harold became lost. He had taken the wrong path. He wasn't sure how he was going to find his way back to the camp but then he came upon a man sitting on a stump. He asked the man for directions.

The man said, "You see that pipe over yonder?"

"Yeah, I see it."

"Well, you follow that pipeline and it will take you back to your car. And when you get back that sun will be going down over the mountain."

Harold didn't enjoy his hunting trip that day. He thought he was lost forever. He was so glad to find his way back to the automobile.

He says, "In those days, when the men were looking for you, they would fire three times and you were supposed to fire back once to answer them. I didn't fire back because I was so close to them but they sure scolded me. They were ready to send someone out looking for me."

The modern appliances that we take for granted today were not to be found in the Bailey's kitchen. One thing, however, made Laura's life more pleasant. They were fortunate to have an icebox. Laura would have to remember to put the sign in the window asking the iceman to stop. Then, she would lug the heavy block of ice and place it in the icebox. It was Harold's job to carry away the melted ice water that had been caught in a bucket under the icebox and empty it into the flower garden. It wasn't the greatest invention ever made but it did keep the milk, butter, and other food cold.

We all make decisions at some point in our lives for which we have failed to consider all of the consequences. Laura had to open a jar while cooking one day and she wasn't strong enough to open it with her hands. For some unknown reason, she tucked the jar under her arm to try to pry it open. To her horror, the jar shattered when she twisted the lid accidentally severing the tendon in her hand that controlled her thumb. It was repaired by surgery satisfactorily but for the woman who made a living with her hands, it made an already stressful life more difficult.

Laura was fanatic about paying her bills on time. No bills could be late. Brownlee Woods, being a residential suburb of Youngstown, had no businesses within its boundaries. There were no banks and the only way to pay the bills was to ride the bus to the center of downtown Youngstown. So rain or shine, she'd hop on the bus and head downtown to take care of her business.

It was a blessing to Laura that her young children gave her no big problems. Or at least she always thought they were little angels. Harold, however, liked to play minor practical jokes on people as he still does today.

He hadn't attended Woodrow Wilson High School very long before the opportunity for his first prank came along. He was walking through Pine Hollow Park on his way to school when he became thirsty. He looked around and there was no place to get a drink of water but he spied a cow in a nearby pasture. Being a country boy, he knew how to milk the cow. He decided that milking the cow could solve the problem. It was a quick way to get a drink and he wouldn't be late for school.

Just as he was enjoying the first squirt of warm milk, the farmer spied him. He chased after Harold, shaking his fist in the air. The farmer was yelling something at him but Harold couldn't make out what he was saying. The farmer wasn't speaking English but Harold's positive that what he said wasn't too pleasant.

Harold's academic experiences with Woodrow Wilson High School weren't much better than were those from his elementary school. He continued to have trouble learning but then he got into woodworking class. That was the only class that he really enjoyed.

The overwhelming pressure on Laura was lessened when Harold became old enough to be able to bring in some money for the household. It was a relief to Harold, too, because it pained him to see his mother work so hard.

Harold worked three jobs at once. One of his first jobs was with a company called the Vahey Marsh Woods Company. He worked with a lot of nice people including his boss who tried to help him whenever he could. Mr. Rashel Walker would always ask him to work odd turns so he could go to school before coming to the factory. Mr. Walker also scheduled his work so he could be sure to leave around 11:30 PM. His second job was working at the McCrory's five and dime store in downtown Youngstown. His third job was making ice at the Ohio Hotel, a famous hotel that existed in Youngstown.

Harold's only transportation to work was the public bus system and the busses quit running at midnight. Guy May was the bus driver on Harold's route. Since Harold was on the bus frequently, Guy and Harold soon became friends. Harold would sit directly behind the driver so they could talk to each other at the end of both of their work shifts.

There was a fairly large woman who just loved to sit next to Harold in the front seat. However, he wanted the seat all to himself or at least to have a little more room than was left after she sat down. He didn't know politely how to tell her that he didn't want her to sit with him so he devised a plan.

The following day, Harold bent a sturdy wire into the shape of a U. He strung a washer onto a rubber band then pulled the ends of the rubber band over the open arms of the U. He centered the washer on the rubber band. He twirled the washer so that the rubber band twisted tightly. He hid the device under his leg and waited for the lady to board the bus.

That night when the lady sat in the seat beside him like he anticipated she would, he lifted his leg. The fluttering sound that the washer made while it rapidly unwound on the bus' leather seat sounded like a natural body function that can be quite odorous at times, the expelling of flatulence.

The lady immediately covered her nose with her handkerchief, said "Oh my God", and walked down the aisle towards the back of the bus. She never sat next to Harold again.

Traveling on the bus brought Harold other laughs during his life. The bus was passing in front of a feed store in Brownlee Woods when a woman flagged it to stop. She jumped on the bus and sat next to Harold. She placed a box on her lap that contained fifteen baby chicks. The baby chicks were making quite a ruckus inside the box even though they were only two or three days old. They were all peeping loudly and scratching the cardboard box bottom with their nails.

There were some children sitting in the seat across the aisle from Harold and the lady. They asked the woman if she would permit them to see the chicks. The lady, thinking that nothing unusual would happen, opened the lid just a crack so that the children could peek in. Out popped three of the chicks running in three different directions.

The lady slammed the box lid shut and shoved the box at Harold. She commanded, "Here, Harold. Hold this." And she ran down the aisle after the three peeps.

She caught two of them at the back of the bus but the third chick ran up front by Guy. As she bent over to catch the third one, "she let out a lot of gas."

Guy laughed and said, "Way to go lady. If you can't catch them, just shoot them."

Harold promises this is a true story. He distinctly remembers her name but he won't divulge that information "because that wouldn't be nice." He said the entire bus was rocking with laughter until she got off. When she did, she looked back, smiled and waved.

The Vahey Marsh Woods Company was the first of three businesses in a row located beside railroad tracks in a valley along with many businesses on the east side of Youngstown. The National Biscuit Company occupied the building beside Vahey Marsh Woods and beside that was the J.V. McNickes Company. All three companies used the railroad for shipping and receiving products.

Harold's job at the Vahey Marsh Woods Company included unloading a railroad tanker car full of high-test gasoline. He and others used a pipe the diameter of a fire hydrant to transfer the gasoline into their facility.

One day as he was unloading the gasoline, Harold noticed some men from the National Biscuit Company jacking up a railroad car that was loaded with crackers. All of a sudden, the railroad car fell off the jack and began rolling down the tracks toward Harold and the gasoline tanker. It coupled onto the gasoline tanker forcing the pipe to jerk out of Harold's hands. The force of the runaway car coupling onto the gasoline tanker caused the railroad cars to roll quickly away, traveling uphill to West Lakes Crossing. When the cars reached West Lakes Crossing, they rolled backwards into the valley and then back up the opposite hill on the other side. They continued to sway back and forth three times like a pendulum.

Gallons upon gallons of gasoline sprayed from the open pipe that was still connected to the tanker car. The gasoline spewed over the entire area.

Workers from both companies tried to stop the rolling cars but the cars were rocking from side to side so intensely that it threw one National Biscuit employee off of the cars. Other employees ran to catch the railroad cars, hoping to apply the brakes. But the brakes weren't working properly.

As it so happened, there was a man inside the National Biscuit Company's boxcar. It was loaded with graham crackers and oyster crackers when the runaway trains careened out of control. All the crackers tumbled on top of the man. He was trapped and at the total mercy of the train until it finally came to a stop on its own.

"He was one salty dude when we finally got him out of there," recalls Harold.

The fire department was called to clean the gasoline from out of the area. Hoping to dilute the fuel, the firemen poured gallons of water on it. They also feared that someone would be so ignorant as to light a match or start any machine that might cause a spark.

Before the cleanup could be started, sightseers converged upon the area from all the nearby neighborhoods. Harold looked at this as an excellent time for another selection from his bag of practical jokes. He puckered his lips and blew a loud whistling sound as if another train was coming down the tracks. The people immediately scattered everywhere looking for the other train.

The railroad company eventually sent another engine to pull the railroad cars to where they needed to be. But that engine's whistle would never cause as panicky a reaction as Harold's had. And after fifty years, Harold's still whistling like a train engine.

Harold's teenage years were a good time in his life. He was finally old enough to be able to travel outside the city limits alone. He would try to arrange each of his work schedules so that he could have one weekly twenty-four hour period free from commitment. And he always tried to plan that day when there was a dance hall or roller skating rink open.

He especially loved roller-skating and did so whenever he could. He felt so carefree as he glided around the rink listening to the music that was filling the air. There weren't too many songs to which he couldn't skate including the waltz and the flea hop.

Harold contributed most of his money towards the household budget leaving little money for fun. But his mother, knowing every worker needs some spending money and recuperation time, said, "Harold, we can afford for you to have twenty-five cents to get into the roller skating rink. Do you want to go there today?'

"Can I have thirty-five cents instead to go to the dance?"

"I don't think we have enough for that but I'll give you an extra dollar to tuck into your wallet in case you run into trouble. Make sure you get a pass from the bus driver so you only have to pay once for the round trip."

Lots of people around him would be eating potato chips or candy but Harold could never afford to purchase any. There was never enough money for the extras we so often take for granted.

At age fourteen or fifteen, he would hop on the bus and go to Idora Park as often as he could. Idora was a big amusement center on the edge of Mill Creek Park just south of Youngstown. A dance hall was located inside Idora Park and he could twirl a lady around the dance floor to big name bands.

Downtown Youngstown offered an exciting event for him once. The President of the United States, Harry S. Truman, visited the area. The town's roads, sidewalks, and buildings had all been cleaned. The local people anticipated the great event for weeks. Everyone who was anyone would be standing on a sidewalk hoping to catch a glimpse of their President as he was driven through the streets.

Harold hitchhiked downtown to be part of the crowd on Poland Avenue. He was absolutely positive that he would be fortunate enough to be able to see one of the most famous men in the country. But all he could see above the crowd was the tip of the president's white scarf flying in the air.

President Truman had come to tour Youngstown's steel mills. The workers were on strike and it was thought that they would destroy millions of dollars worth of company property. In the end, the workers didn't cause as much damage as had been anticipated but the governor had ordered the Ohio Militia to Youngstown in case they were needed to quell any rioting.

The Militia would practice maneuvers every day, first at Buckeye Platt and then on Power's Way, Harold's old sled-riding hill. It was rumored that when they were practicing on Buckeye Platt, the militiamen heard a bugle being played in the distance. It supposedly was disturbing their concentration. One of the officers sent a recruit to determine what was really happening. He allegedly took that bugle away from a ten-year-old boy. It's not known if the bugle was ever returned or if the incident had indeed actually happened.

It was common to observe the Militia stopping railroad tankers before the carloads of oil could enter into the mills. The soldiers would open the lid of each tanker making sure it wasn't being used as a Trojan horse. They had to be sure that there were no men or rifles stowed away in an empty tanker for the purpose of causing a violent outcome inside.

"It was pretty scary in those days for the people in Youngstown," Harold recalls. "Fortunately, those days didn't last long."

When Harold was old enough, his mother finally gave him permission to quit school to obtain a better paying job. He became one of a number of students during the Depression era who were forced to quit school or at least to pause their formal education for the good of the family. It simply wasn't an option for consideration. The extra money was essential for the survival of the family.

The first major decision Laura and Harold made after he quit high school was that it was necessary for him to purchase a vehicle. Laura trusted her sixteen-year-old son to accept the responsibilities she was about to give him. But he would need to obtain his driver's license and car insurance before they could consider spending money on such an expensive luxury. She signed all the necessary papers to allow him to drive and own his first automobile, a 1936 Ford.

CHAPTER SIX

HAROLD'S FIRST TRUE LOVE

Harold's excitement built the entire day through. There was to be a dance in Lordstown that evening and he and his mother had already paid all the household bills for that month. There would be enough money left over so that he could attend the dance. At age 17, he still didn't have the extra money needed to take a date but that didn't deter him. He was a good dancer and he never had any problems finding a dance partner among the ladies who were there.

Upon entering the dance hall, his eyes glanced around the room. Deciding which girl he would ask to be his dance partner for that evening, his gaze stopped on one girl who was standing with some friends by the wall. He was certain she was the same girl he had seen a few times before at basketball games but she was so beautiful he had never had the courage to speak to her. His palms began to sweat. The butterflies in his stomach went on a rampage. But he managed to overcome his fears. He walked what felt like five miles across the dance floor and he asked her to dance.

She had brown silky hair that touched her shoulders. Her cologne smelled heavenly as he led her through the first dance. The curves of her slender body fit perfectly in his. She felt marvelous in his arms. He never wanted to let her go again.

Gazing into her gentle eyes, he wondered to himself why he had never mustered the courage to speak to her at the basketball games. She was so easy to talk to and they had everything in common. She laughed easily at his silly jokes. There were no topics that they disagreed upon. It was as if God had made her specifically for him.

Florence Baker and Harold Bailey formally met on that fateful night in 1946.

Harold says, "We hit it off one, two, three. Seemed like the things we talked about, the things we did, everything was compatible."

During their courtship, they attended many more dances. Ballroom dancing was the prominent style in the mid forties. They liked to dance at the Idora Park Ballroom because many big name bands played there including the Glenn Miller Orchestra and Benny Goodman. They were fortunate to have spun around the floor to Tommy Dorsey's band.

They were so totally in love that it was tempting not to wait but Florence made the decision to attend Kent State University before she became Mrs. Harold Bailey. She knew God's purpose for her on Earth was to become a schoolteacher.

Harold was extremely proud of Florence. To him, she had to be the smartest person in the whole wide world. He didn't even mind that they had to postpone getting married for five years while she finished her education. He would have waited forever as long as she was totally committed to him.

The Bakers thoroughly trusted Harold with the one person who meant the whole world to them, their daughter. They permitted him to bring Florence home from college on weekends and holidays.

Once when Harold was headed to the University, Mr. Baker handed him an envelope. "Harold, this is Florence's tuition. I trust that you will get it to her on time so that it can be paid today. We're a little behind with the payment and all I have is cash so please be careful with it."

Placing the $2,000 in his pocket, Harold's stomach did a few flip-flops. He had been entrusted with every single cent needed to pay for the entire four years of Florence's schooling.

Perhaps because of his nervousness or because his mind was on the weekend to come, Harold took a wrong turn somewhere and he couldn't find his way to the University. The simple flip-flops turned into outright somersaults. He knew Florence would be anxiously awaiting him and he never liked to be late. But he just didn't know which road he had taken that had made him become lost. And he had no idea where he was. He was totally lost.

He drove around and around searching for any landmarks or roads that he could recognize. Nothing looked familiar and he didn't want to ask anyone. He could see from the dilapidated homes that he was in an undesirable neighborhood. And the two thousand dollars in his pocket now felt like a million dollars that he needed to guard even closer.

Somehow he found his way back to State Route 5. He attributes finding the right way to "the good Lord. I might still be lost if I hadn't just had a feeling that I was headed in the right direction. I breathed a sigh of relief when I finally knew that I had found the road heading into Kent."

In the mean time, Florence paced inside the dormitory room checking her watch every few seconds. She looked continually out the windows from wherever she happened to be standing in the room. She had only ten minutes to get her tuition money to the office or she was in danger of being expelled from the University. Chewing on her fingernails, she finally saw Harold pulling into the driveway. She ran out the door and hopped into his 1942 Plymouth. They had only a few minutes to spare before the office closed for the weekend. Florence became the schoolteacher that she always wanted to become.

Harold and Florence finally tied the knot on June 24, 1951. There was a cozy, reverent atmosphere as they exchanged their wedding vows before friends and family in the Lordstown Christian Church on Route 45.

Although Florence was completely devoted to her marriage, she was also devoted to her teaching profession. Her first and only teaching position was in Vernon, Ohio. She began teaching in the two-story building in the fall of 1951.

Harold proudly tells her story as if it occurred only yesterday. "Everyone noticed that she loved teaching children. She also enjoyed all the extra duties associated with the job. People adored her. She was always willing to give the extra time that teachers spend at events outside of a classroom. When teachers were expected to attend an evening PTA meeting, she never complained though others thought they should meet during the day or get additional pay. If a child needed extra help or if the material on the bulletin boards needed replaced with new, she would volunteer immediately. Her friendly smile greeted people at sporting events as she collected the tickets at the door. She was in charge of putting on school plays making sure every student had a part even if it was to just pull the curtain."

He continued. "But Florence was no pushover by her students. When it was their responsibility to do something, they were expected to toe the line. For instance, if a student had missed the school bus, she'd tell them to start walking home. No matter how long the walk or what kind of weather; it was their responsibility to make it home. And it could be a two to ten miles walk from this small country school."

Florence recognized the value of continuing her college education. She spent summers going to workshops and classes. At that time there were no State requirements to renew her teaching license but she knew how much it improved her skills to attend them.

Harold says, "She would register for a convention and she'd actually go there to learn. The trip out of town wasn't the shopping excursion for her that it was for so many other teachers. Perhaps this was one of the reasons that she was such a successful teacher."

They were unable to purchase a large house and Harold had decided it would be more prudent if they bought a farm. A realtor finally found a small one-story house with a barn in Vernon to their liking after searching the communities surrounding Florence's school. The house was situated next to railroad tracks and it wasn't very big but they decided that this small house would become their first home. They may have been poor but they were a strong force together. They became adamant that they would find a way to buy it.

Harold asked the realtor to think of every possible way that they could purchase the farm on West Street, also known as County Road 185. When the realtor wasn't able to provide them with a solution Harold decided to make a visit to the local banker. He inquired if there were any possibilities that the institution would lend money to the newlyweds. At first, there was little hope of that happening.

Then the female banker reconsidered, "If you can raise $500.00 as a down payment, we'll let you have the farm, Mr. Bailey. You must be able to make the monthly payments on it though."

"That's great," Harold exclaimed. "I really don't know how I'll get that much money. But I'll be back. I'll find it somehow."

When Harold walked away from the banker, a gentleman who had been eavesdropping on their conversation approached him. He said, "Harold, I know you're an honest man so I'll lend you the $500.00. You'll have to pay it back but you can take your time. I know you're good for it."

Harold was ecstatic. With only a handshake, he made a pledge to pay that man back as soon as he possibly could.

Evidently, the banker had overheard them. She walked over to Harold and whispered, "Mr. Bailey, did you borrow that money?"

Harold said softly, "Yes I did and I got to pay it back."

"Well," she said, "tomorrow, after all the papers are final and the bank approves your loan, I'll return the amount of the down payment to you."

And true to her word, she refunded the $500.00 to him the next day. Harold immediately ran across the street and paid the neighbor as soon as the money was placed in his hands. He's been forever grateful to the man who helped him get his first big start.

Harold began to join the community organizations right away. He became a member of the Vernon Methodist Church but he did so only to please his wife. His intention was to only sit in the pew on

Sunday mornings and listen to the sermons. However after he had only been attending the services for a few months, he was invited to join the choir. To his total surprise, he agreed to participate. He was also chosen to serve on the Church Board and to call the numbers for the Church's bingo games. His life became closely entwined with Church functions and he loved it.

The Vernon Methodist Church has an unusual tradition. Harold doesn't know exactly when the tradition was begun but he thinks it was around 1800. Whenever major political elections are held such as voting for President of the United States, the congregation cooks a huge meal and invites the public to join them for dinner. Harold testifies that they cook the best food around. The menu may consist of French fried oysters or homemade vegetable soup or fried chicken or all three main dishes. Baked potatoes with gravy and coleslaw are also served. And if anyone's still hungry, they can slather warm homemade bread with gobs of creamy butter for that 'stick to the ribs' feeling. The meal is strictly self-serve so if anyone wants to eat, they have to dish it onto their own plate.

Harold raised hogs on their farm for meat for the family meals and to sell them to other people. He would raise about a hundred at one time and when they weren't in their pens inside the barn, they were allowed to roam freely around the acreage.

Railroad tracks ran across the back of Harold's farm. Harold, being neighborly, liked to talk with the men who worked on the railroad and they became friends. Harold would warn them when he was going to turn the hogs loose from the barn.

"Hey friend, I'm putting the hogs out today. Is this a good time?"

"Can you wait a few days? We're gonna' be putting up some fence and it will take that long."

"It's gonna' be hard but I'll keep them in the barn a few days. I'll help you out."

Harold knew it could be dangerous if one of his hogs happened to wander onto the railroad tracks. When a train hits a hog, the hog more than likely becomes stuck underneath a railroad car causing the train to derail.

About fifty men working together erected the fence as quickly as they could. The metal-link fence was graded having openings from approximately two inches square at the bottom to four inches square at the top. The small openings at the bottom made the fence stronger and the smaller holes could keep animals from wandering onto the train tracks. The larger openings at the top unfortunately served as a trap for larger animals if they tried to jump over the fence.

It became a part of Harold's daily routine to check the fence for animals. If deer tried to jump the fence, they wouldn't be able to lift their back feet high enough to clear the top. Their feet would become entangled in the fence and they would need to be set free. And deer were plentiful on the sixty-acre farm.

When Harold found a deer caught in the fence, he'd think, 'Oh, oh. He's eaten. Why, he's already caught. I don't need a gun or nothing else. He's not going nowhere.'

Some of the deer that became caught were lucky. When they were still alive, Harold would set them free as he made his rounds checking the farm.

On an autumn day, a hunter came up to Harold and asked, "Would you mind if we take that deer that got stuck in your fence? We have been driving deer and we recognize it as being one that we were hunting."

"Go ahead and take it friend. I have plenty of meat in my freezer," said Harold.

But Harold warns us all, "You can't fuss around. You got to know what you're doing, you know. An animal that's cornered can be very dangerous."

A large German plum tree grew in the side yard of their Vernon farm. The large plums were dark purple and the sweetest plums Harold had ever eaten. But for some unknown reason, the fruit from his tree fell to the ground before it became ripe. Harold compared his plum tree with others around the neighborhood. The fruit on his neighbor's trees remained on the branches until it was picked or until someone shook the tree. Harold couldn't determine what made the trees different so he decided to do some investigating.

Finally, one woman told him the cause. She said, "Mr. Bailey, this is what you do. You measure up six inches from the bottom of the tree and you drive a 6-penney nail into the tree. Then you go around to the other side and you go up six inches. You drive another 6-penney nail into the tree. That tree is lacking iron."

And he did just that to his tree. He swears the lady knew exactly what she was talking about. The following year after he pounded 6-penney nails into his German plum tree and every year after that he couldn't shake those plums off the tree.

While resting in his favorite easy chair one afternoon, Harold heard the explosive sound of metal hitting metal and the crackling sound of shattering glass. He jumped from the chair and pulled back the curtains from the windows to be able to see what had happened. He saw that a train had struck a pick-up truck.

He grabbed his hunting jacket and ran outside to the accident about '90 miles an hour'. There was nothing he could do to help the people and he noticed that the train had been carrying a load of butter. There was one damaged railroad car that was completely filled with the delicacy.

The train engineer, recognizing him, yelled, "Help yourself, Bailey. It'll just melt out here."

Harold stuffed the pockets of his jacket with the precious butter and took it to his home. He returned to get as much as he could carry but he reconsidered what he was doing. He thought maybe it would be better to ask permission from someone higher in authority than the engineer since he "never believes in taking anything that doesn't belong to him."

He found the railroad detective and said, "My name is Harold Bailey and I live right over there on that farm. I came over and got two great big bunches of butter."

The detective looked at him and said, "Well, why don't you go over there and get some more. The insurance company will take care of this."

And Harold did. However, he didn't have a freezer in his refrigerator and he didn't have a cool place in which to store a lot of butter. He didn't want to waste any of the commodities and he also wanted to share this opportunity so he loaded more blocks of butter into the backseat of his car. He passed it out to each of his neighbors until everyone in the neighborhood had more butter than they could use.

He then telephoned his relatives living in Lordstown and said he'd be right out with some butter for them. After hanging up the receiver, he became concerned about carrying that much extra weight in his automobile. He had already loaded several bricks into the car and could see that there might be trouble driving it. Each brick of butter weighed only one pound but his car was already leaning at an angle from the additional weight. He checked the tires and his shocks. He finally determined that there really weren't any problems. The car was able to carry the heavy load and he drove to Lordstown to share the extra butter with his family.

CHAPTER SEVEN

THE FAIRY TALE ENDS

Life for Florence and Harold was a fairy tale. They lived in a white farmhouse that they loved. Donald, their first child, was born on July 29, 1954 three years after their wedding. And almost three years after that on May 28, 1957, they were blessed with a daughter, Kari Sue. Everything in their world was like living in a dream and it seemed like nothing could possibly get any better for them. But soon, tragedy struck for the young couple.

The day was a perfect one to go to a beach. The sky was azure blue with only a few wispy clouds floating by. The sun was shining warmly and Harold and Florence decided that a trip to Lake Erie would make a great family outing. It would only take them about forty-five minutes to get there and they could stay until after dark if they wanted. Florence was on summer vacation and she convinced Harold that the farm would be alright if he only fed the hogs that day.

They had a "beautiful day". Donnie ran along the beach, dug deep holes in the scratchy sand that filled with the lake's water, and built sand castles with his dad's help.

They all braved Lake Erie's frigid water allowing Kari Sue's feet to experience their first waves. After they finished wading and swimming, the tasty picnic lunch quieted the grumbling noises in their stomachs.

It seemed as if Florence was constantly busy with the children that entire summer day allowing little time for resting. The curious three-year-old, Donnie, was continually asking the question "Why?" to everything she said. Kari Sue needed fed and her diaper changed every few hours. Florence needed to watch the children constantly so they didn't hurt themselves or venture too close to the water.

Florence loved each and every minute she spent with her family that day. The summer would soon come to an end and school would be starting. She would miss not cuddling her babies and waiting on Harold but teaching always rejuvenated her spirit.

Around 9 o'clock that night after a totally blissful but exhausting day, the lively toddler and the active baby were tucked into bed. Florence could finally soak in a warm refreshing bath and then retire for the night. She didn't feel all that well but she attributed her achiness to pure exhaustion. The soothing water and a good night's rest would take care of any of the discomfort that she was feeling.

Lying on the bed's cool sheets felt heavenly. Her thoughts began to drift. She thought how peaceful it felt to snuggle in her husband's arms as she slipped into a deep sleep.

The next morning, Harold awoke with a start. An eerie silence filled the room. He sat upright in their bed, his eyes adjusting to the dim dawning light. He wondered what had awakened him and why there were no sounds in the room. He couldn't see anything wrong.

He gazed lovingly down at his wife thinking how much she meant to him. He lightly ran his hand over her arm being careful not to wake her. Florence was so still but she had been totally exhausted from the trip to the beach. She felt cold as she lie beside him. He pulled the blankets from the foot of the bed thinking he'd cover her to take away her chill.

Then it suddenly occurred to him. It was August 14. One of the hottest months of the year. She shouldn't be so cold. He instantly became wide-awake and bolted out of bed to turn on the bright lights.

He immediately saw that she didn't look right. Her face was pale and her lips were tinged a ghastly bluish purple color. Placing his ear on her nightgown, he couldn't hear her heart beating. He shook her and shouted Florence's name but she never stirred.

Harold's mind wasn't able to focus on what he should be doing. Should he run to his neighbors for help? Should he telephone for an ambulance? Should he call her parents first? He felt totally alone in their house yet he had to do something before the children awoke. He had to protect his children. He had to get help but the whirlwind in his mind wouldn't allow him to think about whom he should be calling first. He was having difficulty putting together a reasonable thought. He couldn't stop his head from reeling. He was suddenly dizzy and afraid that he might faint. But he had to do something.

He finally calmed enough to decide to first call for an ambulance. Even though it had been only several minutes after he had found his beloved Florence, the men arrived too late to revive her that morning in 1957.

His second call was to Florence's parents. They must be told at once. It was one of the most difficult calls he ever had to make in his life. They assured him that they would come immediately to the house to be with him and the children.

Harold's thoughts flew back to the time when he was told that his father had died. He didn't know how he could spare his children from such horrific pain. There was no earthly way.

He had no idea what to do next. Should he be doing something or did he already do everything he needed to at that moment? Harold wished someone else were there to relieve him of the insurmountable weight that had suddenly appeared on his shoulders.

Florence's parents arrived and drove Harold to Trumbull Memorial Hospital in Warren, Ohio while the neighbors watched the children. He couldn't give the Bakers any answers to their questions. She had seemed fine when she came to bed the night before. They had spent a great day together. She was tired but who wouldn't be after playing all day in the fresh air?

After sitting and waiting for what seemed an interminable time, they saw the doctor approaching them. "Harold, Mr. and Mrs. Baker. I'm sorry but there was nothing we could do. She was already gone and she more than likely passed away some time early this morning."

They had been married only six short years when Harold's beloved Florence passed away. They had no way of knowing that a rare heart condition had claimed this young wife and mother while the 28-year-old woman lie sleeping beside her husband in their marriage bed.

The doctor continued, "We aren't exactly sure why Florence died so suddenly. I'd like to have an autopsy performed to determine the exact cause of death."

Harold cried, "No. I can't let you hurt my Florence any more. You can't bring her back. Let her rest in peace."

"Now, Harold, let's think about this a minute," Mr. Baker cried in agony. "We all know how deeply you loved our daughter. But we need to know what happened to Florence. Please, we're begging you. Let the doctors find out what went wrong. She was so young. She seemed to be in perfect health and now she's gone. None of us can understand it."

" I can't think," Harold sobbed. "I don't know if I can stand to have my beautiful Florence cut apart. Please give me a little time to think about it."

"We can understand how you're feeling. This is extremely difficult for us, too. But Harold, the doctors said they might be able to help someone else. Don't you think it would be worth saving someone else's life? We really think Florence would want it that way."

Harold thought 'this is so hard. What would Florence want? Maybe she would agree with her parents. She was always the first to jump up and help others. If the doctor really thinks it would benefit someone else, I guess that's what Florence would have wanted.' And then he said aloud, "I'll agree to the autopsy. What do I have to do? What do I have to sign?"

The autopsy revealed a condition that was unexpected. Florence had passed away from a rare type of heart condition known as non-suppurative myocarditis. It was the final punishment to her body from three different infections that were present at the same time. They were severe infections that ravaged her body but remained totally hidden to her. Harold was told that her doctors later recorded this rarity in medical journals.

The autopsy was Harold's and Florence's final unselfish gift to the world together. Ultimately, Florence did help doctors to heal other people.

Harold and the family members decided that the children were too young to be taken to the funeral home. Everyone thought that they really wouldn't understand what was happening anyway. They all felt that it was better to protect them from the weeping and the dark oppressive atmosphere that hung heavily in the air. Therefore, the children were not present when the young, beautiful wife and mother was laid to rest.

Harold's grief consumed him but he managed somehow to get through the next few days. It seemed like he was wandering around in a dense haze and he needed help parting the vast gray veil that covered his world. But he knew he had to try to go on with the business of living. He had two young children to care for.

CHAPTER EIGHT

EVERYTHING JUST WENT BACKWARDS

"Isn't it wonderful you don't know what lies ahead of us?" exclaims Harold today. "You might not have the courage to go on if we did know."

Harold soon found that the children became confused and irritable. They demanded more and more of their father's attention. He gave every extra ounce of energy to them that he could muster and every extra minute of his time but it never seemed like enough. He questioned his ability to take care of his family without a wife. How much longer could he go on without a mother for his children? How could he possibly work at his job, take care of their farm, and take care of a small baby and a young toddler?

And then the crying began. Donnie, just three years old, missed his mother. He wandered through the house hour by hour searching for the mother he couldn't find. He searched for her in the kitchen. He looked in the living room and in the bedrooms. He begged his daddy to go get her. He watched outside the screen door every day to see if she was working in the garden. The little son couldn't understand why his mother was not pulling into the driveway, coming home to them after a trip to the grocery store.

Night after night when it became bedtime, Donnie sobbed even harder for his mother. He needed her to kiss him goodnight but she wouldn't come to him. He wanted her to read him the stories he loved to hear but he couldn't find her. Why wasn't she beside his bed? Why couldn't he hear her coming to snuggle his blankets under his chin?

Harold's heart ached as he watched the streams of tears escaping from Donnie's eyes. Harold cried when he watched his son sobbing for so long that his little teeth chattered. The crying lasted for what seemed like entire nights through but Harold just didn't know how to help his son understand that he couldn't bring his mother to him.

Harold tried to comfort him but all his efforts were to no avail. Donnie needed the comfort only a mother can give. Harold was at a loss as to what to do for his small son.

Harold questioned every word he had said and every action he had taken from the moment he found Florence's lifeless body. But there really were no answers. He wondered if perhaps Donnie had seen her or touched her coolness while she lay in her coffin if it might have been easier for him to understand.

Harold continues to agonize over his decision today. "Maybe it was a mistake that I didn't take him to the funeral home. Maybe he wasn't too young to understand. Maybe if I had held my son in my arms and explained quietly what happened to his mother while we looked at her? Maybe Donnie would have known then that he would never see his mother again."

Harold became totally exhausted. He was being awakened off and on all night long. He worked eight hours at the mill during the day and three to four hours in the evening doing the farm chores. Between providing for his family and taking care of Kari Sue and Donnie, there was little time for rest to chase away his weariness and depression. It was almost impossible for him to go on without his wife. He was near collapsing when his father-in-law approached him.

"Harold, don't you think it's time we take Donnie to a doctor? Maybe the doctor will know something we can do to help him get over this rough time."

"Perhaps we'd better. We gotta' get him straightened out."

The doctor empathized with Harold's plight. He could see the toll that the exhaustion was taking upon him. He thought there was only one solution.

"The only thing you can do is to change Donnie's scenery. That means you've got to move. You've got to change everything around that boy. It's going to be tough, but it has to be done."

"I understand," Harold reluctantly agreed.

But it was unbearable for Harold to leave his farm no matter how alone and desperate he was feeling. The memories that haunted Donnie were the ones that comforted Harold. The chair that Florence sat in, the empty place beside him in bed, the spot on the floor where she always stood to wash the dishes were all reminders of the once perfect life that they had shared.

It was also difficult for him to sell the property that he had worked so hard to purchase. He was proud of what he had accomplished and he would have to give it away to strangers. But he would do anything to make his son feel better and the doctor told him that it was the only thing he could do.

The move couldn't happen quickly though. Harold had no place to take his family and he had no strength to make the decisions on his own. He had to go through his grief and help himself before he could become strong enough to help his children. To Harold, every hope, every dream in his life that had been promised to be fulfilled, "just went backwards."

CHAPTER EIGHT

BEGINNING AGAIN

He needed to get away from his thoughts if only for an hour or two. He recalled his father saying every new broom sweeps clean and knew he had to get back to the business of truly living. Dances once again lured Harold back into the social world. He had always enjoyed this sport and he knew the chances were good that there would be friendly people at any dance hall he picked. And he needed to be surrounded by happy people in an upbeat atmosphere. His mental health depended upon it.

Always having a special intuition about people, Harold knew right away if he liked and trusted someone to be a good person. Elsie Hunter Bieber was one of those "someones." He wondered what people would think if he invited her to a dance. He wondered if it was too soon after Florence's death. But he no longer could live a lonely life. He made the major decision to invite her to a dance.

He felt like he was 18 once again. Why would a grown man feel so nervous about a simple date? His knees were wobbly and he felt sweat rolling down the middle of his back. Would he be brave enough to kiss her goodnight? Should he even be so bold as to try to kiss her goodnight? He wanted to make a good impression. He didn't want to ruin his chances with this woman. He felt that familiar knot in the pit of his stomach that said Elsie Bieber was a special lady.

He timidly knocked on her door. His mouth was as dry as the Sahara Desert. He started to speak but his lips stuck together as if they were glued. He attempted to lick them but he couldn't find one drop of moisture to wet his sandpapery tongue. Where had all the water gone that normally made his mouth as moist as an oasis in that desert?

She gave him a knowing smirk. She was having the same thoughts as Harold. She felt like a giddy schoolgirl going on her first date rather than an adult who had been married before.

He gallantly escorted her to his car and opened the door. He gazed at the smile on her delicate face, the face that seemed to glow in the moonbeams. Her dark hair brushed softly against his arm as she slid onto the seat. A slight smile formed on his lips as he watched her pull her shapely legs inside. She positioned herself on the car seat comfortably.

Harold thought he had noticed everything about her. But what he hadn't noticed was that she hadn't had time to take her hand away from the doorframe. Harold closed the door. He closed the door tightly on her fingers.

He heard her blood-curdling scream as he turned to walk away towards his side of the car. He rushed back, yanking open the car door. He got a sickening, nauseated feeling as he looked at the slender hand that he had just injured.

It was one of the most excruciating pains anyone could experience. It was also one that a person never forgets. Older model automobiles were designed so that there was no extra space between the door and the doorframe. When a car door was shut inadvertently with someone's fingers resting on the door's center post, and it happened often, the fingers became flattened and grotesque looking. No matter how quickly one yanked open the door, the fingers and/or their nails invariably turned dark purple from bruising almost instantly. And one was lucky if they weren't broken.

Harold felt horrified. He had hurt the one person he was trying to impress the most. He worried that she might never speak to him again.

Harold adopted the philosophy that when bad things happen to him, they were meant to happen for a reason. And he was right again.

Elsie did speak to Harold again, several times. It wasn't long after he totally bumbled their first date that Elsie's girlfriend remarked, "I can see that I'm losing another girlfriend. I can see her falling in love with Harold Bailey."

As Harold began to know more about Elsie, he discovered that she was quite a bit older than him, ten years as a matter of fact. But he didn't mind. He had come to the conclusion early in his teens that he preferred women that were older than him. He found that they were easier to be around than women his own age.

"They're old enough to have some intelligence and they've had some experience with life. Why, their elevator goes clear to the tenth floor," chuckles Harold.

Harold was thinking that every new broom sweeps clean and he wondered if it was time to ask Elsie to marry him. He didn't have to worry about her answer.

Elsie's best friends were Betty and Buster Mounts from New Springfield, Ohio. After Harold met them, they became his good friends also. "We got along like two peas in a pod." The two couples became so close that Harold and Elsie asked Betty and Buster to be the matron of honor and best man at their wedding.

The wedding ceremony was held in 1958 with a few friends and family in the congregation. They were married in the Vernon Methodist Church on Route 7 in Vernon, Ohio.

A small luncheon was served after the ceremony at the Octagon House in Kinsman, the home of Attorney Clarence Darrow. The celebrating was continued after lunch at their farm in Vernon.

After a fashionable time, the newlyweds packed their suitcases and headed for their honeymoon to upper Michigan. Thanks to the children's grandparents, Harold and Elsie could leave all of the children and responsibilities at home. They had a wonderful vacation free from worries.

CHAPTER NINE

COMBINING FAMILIES

Combining households can prove to be rather difficult but Elsie with Harold's assistance was determined to make it happen smoothly. Both of them willingly and excitedly accepted the challenge. For them, the best was yet to come.

Harold and Elsie's family evolved into the stereotypical home of the 1950's. Elsie had never held a job and it wasn't necessary for her to enter the work world now. She didn't know how to drive a car and she didn't need to learn. The 50's woman's role was to stay home and to take care of the tasks inside the house. Elsie also handled the greater share of raising the children including the discipline. It was Harold's duty to provide money for the family and to take care of the outside of the home.

Having an abundance of love to share, Elsie and Harold accepted each other's children as if they were their own. But that's not to say that there weren't a few complications along the way.

Elsie's sons were practically raised. They hadn't had a father in their lives for quite a while. Howard, Elsie's oldest son at eighteen years old, was married and had already left home. Richard, Elsie's youngest son, thought of himself as a young adult as do all teenagers at fourteen years of age. He was entering the time in his life when teenagers frequently test a parent's rules. To add to the stress of fighting for his independence, he had been taken out of his school and away from his friends.

Elsie, being ten years older than Harold, hadn't had small children in her house for a long time. Harold's children, Donnie and Kari Sue were virtually babies. Naturally being rambunctious, little ones can be physically draining for a woman at any age. Children that small can also cause emotional turmoil for any woman and especially for a woman who thinks her child-rearing days are almost over. To take on the challenge of raising a four year old with abandonment problems and a baby that's one and a half years old, some would say that Elsie was a saint. Others would say that she was just a woman who dearly loved children.

Harold's relatives came to question how Elsie was attending to Kari Sue. It's said that they thought Elsie loved Kari Sue so deeply that she spent the greater part of her day carrying Kari Sue on her hip. They became convinced that Kari Sue would never learn to walk unless Elsie gave her the opportunity to learn. The relatives, in a subtle manner, pleaded with Elsie to rethink her ways. She finally agreed to put Kari Sue on the floor for longer periods of time. She would no longer carry her continually. She would allow her to begin taking the necessary steps in learning how to walk. It didn't take long for Elsie and the relatives to watch Kari Sue toddle off on her own.

Harold gloats with pride when talking about Elsie's sons, the stepsons he thinks of as his own. One would never know they weren't his biological children unless he told you.

He says, "Both boys are very, very intelligent because they've taken after their parents. Maybe it's a good thing they really aren't my flesh and blood."

Howard Bieber became an electrician. Harold says he's an expert when it comes to wiring and electrical things. Howard's brother agrees.

Dick became a building contractor. Harold jokes that Dick has brains that he hasn't used yet. When told about that statement, Dick smiled and reluctantly agreed with Harold's assessment. Dick loves to use his hands and he loves to build houses. His beautiful two-story home built close to Elsie and Harold's is proof of his ability.

Elsie and her sons had sacrificed her home in Boardman to move to Vernon to be with Harold. But they soon came to know that their family was destined to live in that house only a short time. Donnie continued to cry frequently at night over the loss of his mother. Elsie had a difficult time comforting him and the almost constant turmoil was upsetting to the entire family.

Elsie finally told Harold, "We have to do something for that poor baby. I think it's time that we take the doctor's advice and find new surroundings for Donnie.

I'd like to go look around Boardman and see if there is anything we would like to buy."

Harold says, "We were poor, as poor as hen's teeth and that's pretty poor."

But they both knew that it was time to try something else. All the other solutions had failed. They now knew they had to totally change Donnie's surroundings if Donnie was to ever get through his grief. They hoped that by removing the physical objects, Donnie's only memories of his mother would dim and life would become more tolerable for him.

Harold always says every new broom sweeps clean and it was time to start sweeping.

Harold and Elsie found an old house with a run-down barn in North Lima. They thought they might be able to afford it. Harold was fairly certain he could renovate the house so they could live comfortably in it. He knew he could fix the barn to be serviceable.

Harold went to the bank in Vernon and approached the banker for a loan. The banker asked, "Do you have any money, Mr. Bailey?"

"No. I don't have any money."

"H-m-m. Well, come on. Let's go to the back room and talk about this."

Closing the door, the banker said, "Let me give you some advice. Borrow all the money you can borrow and go down and buy that farm. When you sell your farm here in Vernon, sell it on a land contract. Make sure that guy pays you enough money every month to make the payments on a bank loan. That way you won't have to worry about paying your monthly payments on the new farm."

Harold sold his Vernon farm including his livestock almost immediately to a reliable family. There were no problems with the family meeting the mandatory deadlines for the Vernon farm. Therefore, Harold was able to make the payments on the North Lima farm every month and on time.

Purchasing the new farm turned out to be the easiest part of this new venture in Harold's life. Moving his family from Vernon to North Lima, over a fifty-mile distance, proved to be the most challenging. Harold didn't have enough money to hire anyone to move their belongings nor did he have the extra funds to rent a moving van for the day. But for him, where there's a will, there's a way and he was determined to get the move done in one day. It may not have been under the best conditions but Harold's solution was the only option open to him.

He strapped the furnishings from their house and all of their clothes onto two sixteen-foot hay wagons. He then hitched the wagons behind his farm tractor. All their worldly possessions would ride easily on the two wagons for the move to North Lima.

Harold began the journey early in the morning. Elsie packed a few sandwiches for him to eat along the way. Kissing her goodbye, he placed them in his pocket.

Harold says he owned one of the fastest tractors in those days, a Co-op. It had rubber tires not wire or metal and "they were pretty centrally located" so the tractor didn't sway from side to side. It was steady enough that he was able to stand up without falling while the tractor was moving. When there were no cars coming towards him or trying to pass him, "I'd crank that baby into 4th gear and go fairly fast." He guesses he was traveling about 15 or 20 miles per hour.

Harold recalls that he filled the tractor with gasoline and placed an additional five-gallon can filled with gasoline on one of the hay wagons. As he was putting the gallon container on the wagon, he remembered his father telling him that one gallon of gasoline is equal to seven sticks of dynamite.

He speculates that if some semi-truck or car had hit him, "Pow! You'd have read about it in the paper. There wouldn't have been anything left. I don't know why the good Lord does things but He made that trip safe and sound."

It took all day for Harold to travel the fifty miles to their new farm. And he says he didn't stop for anything. When he got hungry, he ate his sandwiches that he had stuffed in his pockets and drove at the same time. He had to get to North Lima before dark.

Moving day for the Baileys became another family event. Mr. and Mrs. Baker, Florence's parents, volunteered to drive the rest of the family to the new farm. Other relatives came to drive Harold's car. All in all it was a tiring day for everyone but the Bailey family got moved into its new home and was ready to begin its new life.

Once they got settled in their house and were able to neighbor with people, they all found that they fit in with the others as if they had always lived there. It was a "good feeling" for Harold because he felt a little uneasy and somewhat guilty about uprooting Elsie's son once again.

The first snowfall to come to North Lima, an area that tends to be in the snowbelt area of eastern Ohio, reminded Harold that he had another job to do. The driveway, approximately 150-200 feet long, needed to have the wrath of winter removed from it. His job was to improvise a snowplow somehow.

His plow was rather crude compared to today's models. There was no windshield or other protection from the cold snow and blowing winds. However, Harold thought his invention worked well and he was only too happy to plow all of the neighbor's driveways when he was finished with his.

Since Harold never liked to be late for anything, he'd rise from his warm, toasty bed at four o'clock in the morning on snowy days to begin plowing. He swears the weather was much worse in those days and weather statistics support his claim. The snowfalls were oftentimes deeper and the temperatures were colder. He'd plow all the snow he possibly could before going to work at Youngstown Sheet and Tube Steel Mill.

He's proud that he was only late six times in all of the thirty years that he worked at the mill. Once, his tardiness was beyond his control during the winter. His car got a flat tire on the driver's side of the car while driving to work and he "had his hands full." The cars on the road were traveling about 45-55 miles an hour. He managed to pull the car off to the side of the wet slushy road to change the tire. Kneeling down to take care of the problem, the back of his coat became splattered with filthy slush thrown from the other cars' tires as they sped behind him on the road. His hands became bitter cold and he didn't own any gloves. He replaced the flat tire as fast as he possibly could and continued on to work.

After they had lived in North Lima a short while, a pleasant surprise happened. The man who bought the Vernon farm called Harold on the telephone. "Harold, I'm ready to pay off my loan."

"Are you sure? There's no rush and you'd be paying it off ahead of time."

"I can't wait to own my property free and clear. Can we meet at the bank tomorrow?"

"We sure can. I'll be there."

Harold went to Elsie with a proposition. "Would it be agreeable with you to refund the man a little bit of money for paying off the loan early?"

They decided that they could give the man $500.00, the exact amount lent to Harold when he purchased the home.

Harold E Bailey
The Friendly trapper

On a routine "trap check", Harold finds a raccoon as he strolls in the woods on his property.

Trapper removes a hornets' nest from bushes. Hope it's plugged well!

The Trapper and his truck have seen many a mile!

Varmints and critters are his love and calling

Bailey won't come home until he helps you trap those pests

Harold E. Bailey, known as the Friendly Trapper, stresses nonlethal pest-control methods. He has written a book, gives talks on pest control and has a radio show.

KAREN SCHIELY/Akron Beacon Journal

The Grotto Clowns

Left - Beth Johnson
Right - Lindsey Rogers

Harold says, "It made me feel so good. I was at long last able to financially help another person. I felt that the Lord provided a way for me to do God's work."

CHAPTER ELEVEN

A SAMPLE OF HOME LIFE

Harold's life with Elsie was measured one loving day at a time. He absolutely adored her and he let everyone know it. He talked often of how fantastic a cook she was. He loved every delicious morsel and was totally convinced that she could cook anything to perfection.

Harold continues to rave to this day, "She could turn a tough old chicken into a tender moist banquet to be enjoyed. She could cook wild game such as pheasant and rabbit. That's not easy to do and it takes special preparation and spices to make it taste just right. She could even make it so that people who had never eaten wild game before couldn't guess what it was. They ate it and loved it."

Elsie's love of cooking prompted Harold to look for anything that she could turn into a feast. Harold loved to pick blackberries to take home to her. He would attach a makeshift handle to a three pound coffee can. He'd hang the can from his belt leaving both hands free to pick without any barriers. It didn't take long for the entire can to become filled with black juicy berries.

"Elsie would turn those berries into one of her works of perfection. She would bake several flaky pies, perhaps fifteen, at one time. She then froze them along with any leftover berries for another day."

The Baileys had a total of seven freezers in their home at one time. Harold not only bought them to store extra food but to comfort Elsie. She was petrified of running out of food. Her son thought her feelings may have been a throwback to the depression era when there was never enough food for her family. No matter the reason, Harold loved to keep his wife happy so he did whatever he could to keep her that way.

On many Sunday afternoons after arriving home from church, Elsie would pop a frozen blackberry pie into the oven to heat. While it was baking, the rest of the family made homemade vanilla ice cream to dollop onto huge slices of the warm mouth-watering pie. Harold would begin cranking the paddles of the old-fashioned ice cream maker. The boys would take over when the sweet cream began to thicken and the paddles seemed like they couldn't possibly be turned any more.

When the cream, sugar, eggs, and vanilla were finally churned into ice cream, the boys were forced to draw straws. The best flavor of the ice cream in the crock would be wound in and around the metal paddles and they all wanted the chance to lick them clean. The winner was the one who picked the shortest straw of all the ones Harold held in his hand.

Harold also enjoyed picking elderberries for Elsie. He combed the woods and fields around their home for the huge bushes loaded with fruit in the spring. He'd pick buckets full of the purple clusters so that Elsie could cook them into jams, jellies, sauces, and pies.

He found a slick way to remove the B.B. sized berries from their stem. He'd rake the tines of a fork from the top of the stem outwards towards the berries like combing someone's hair. Those elderberries would fall off into his pan in no time at all.

Harold says he used to watch women fighting to clean the clusters of elderberries. They'd pick each tiny elderberry off the stem by hand and consequently their hands became stained dark purple from the elderberry juice. He says however that he didn't really mind when his own hands looked like they'd been dipped in gallons of juice. He'd just lick it off because it tasted so darn good.

Another favorite dish that Elsie made was homemade cottage cheese and apple butter. Elsie's recipe for the apple butter called for seven different kinds of apples: Baldwin, Red Delicious, Yellow Delicious, Winesap, Roman Beauty, and another one that Harold can't recall. She'd plop tablespoonfuls of the delicacy onto a small mound of smearcase, as cottage cheese was called, and it would become an instant dessert.

Harold and Elsie liked to travel north to Lake Erie to pick cherries in the early summer. They'd drive along Lake Erie on Route 2 watching the waves rolling on the water. They would stop at one of the many beaches along the way and enjoy the cool breezes drifting in from the lake as well as stopping at their favorite orchards. They picked the larger cherries named Queen Anne and Black Cherry.

As they were picking cherries off a tree, a man began chatting with them. "My wife and I have a favorite recipe to use some of those sweet cherries. Are you interested in knowing how to make them?"

"Sure friend. What's your secret?"

"Leave the stems on the cherries when you're picking them. When you get home, put the cherries into a bottle of Vodka and place it in your freezer."

"Won't that bottle break when I put it in the freezer? It's gonna' swell up and we'll have a big ole' mess," said Harold.

"Now think about what you're asking me. Vodka is 82 proof," the man said.

"Oh, yeah," Harold remembered, "alcohol doesn't freeze."

Harold and Elsie weren't sure if they would follow the recipe or not but they thanked the man for telling them about it. On the way home, they decided they would give it a try.

"Those cherries tasted so garwsh darn good but it's a taste that's hard to describe. And we had to watch how many we ate. Why, we could get drunk if we ate too many."

Harold, being the jokester that he is, devised another trick when they had company and it was people that they knew fairly well. This time he lured Elsie into being his cohort.

One Thanksgiving, a lady with exceptionally high moral standards came to visit. She was a tea-totaler and never touched a drop of alcoholic beverages nor put a morsel of wild game in her mouth. It was a perfect time for a joke if Harold ever saw one.

Elsie placed the alcohol-soaked cherries in a dish and set the cherries on the dinner table. The lady wasn't able to taste that the fruit had been 'sabotaged' as she popped cherry after cherry into her mouth. She obviously was becoming more and more inebriated. Harold and Elsie didn't have the courage to tell her that they had been soaked in Vodka even when they decided that the joke had gone on long enough. And she just wouldn't leave them alone. Elsie relented to not putting any more cherries in the dish because the prim, proper lady wouldn't quit eating them.

Harold swears that their guest began talking to herself within a short time. He still breaks out in sidesplitting laughter when he thinks about her getting a 'little buzz' from the Vodka.

Harold was always supported by Elsie in anything he did. It was important to Harold and he always appreciated the fact that Elsie was "always around me. We'd go to church and she'd be right along my side."

The only time they didn't go to church together was when Harold would have to go to work. Sometimes he had to work a sixteen-hour shift at the mill and sometimes he would be called in to work on his day off. During those times, their neighbors gladly took Elsie to church since she didn't drive.

Harold fondly remembers Elsie sitting in their living room, watching television and sewing. The television had a small screen because it was all they could afford but she loved to watch it.

Harold would watch his wife working on one of her favorite hobbies, sewing quilts. He marveled that her stitches were always the same even length, which is difficult for an amateur quilter to accomplish.

Elsie made quilts that she entered into competitions. She often won prizes for the handwork she had painstakingly sewn into them. The children wanted Elsie to sell some of her quilts to make extra money. They were convinced that her beautiful quilts were worth a tremendous amount of money. But they could never convince her to sell her contest winners.

It was mutually agreed that in their marriage, Harold was the head of the household. Being the boss, Harold had a special way of dealing with any conflicts that would arise. He would call a "board meeting" and bring the feuding parties together. He appointed himself as the mediator. For instance, if there were a disagreement between his children, Donnie and Kari Sue, he'd call the two offenders to the table.

"Come on. Sit down at the table. I'm calling a Board Meeting."

He didn't always agree with the outcome but the argument was settled. And hopefully the argument had been settled once and for all.

When Donald was seventeen years old, he walked in the door a little late from a date. Harold sternly asked, "Where's your car, Donnie?"

"Uh, Dad," Donnie mumbled, "I'm sorry I'm late but I have a little problem. I was coming around the bend and I accidentally went into the neighbor's pasture. Right through the barbed wire," he answered with his chin almost resting on his chest.

"You know what your problem was?" asked Harold. "You were squeezing her too tight."

Calming down, Harold continued, "Well, come on, son. Let's go take care of your problem."

Together they went to the barn and fired up the dependable Co-op tractor. They threw a log chain and a cable onto the back of the tractor and went to get the car. Fortunately, the car hadn't traveled too far off the road.

Harold told Donnie, "Now, you go to the owner and tell him you're sorry. You say that you tore down his fence and could he keep his cattle out of his pasture until you can fix it. And then you'll go back tomorrow and you'll fix that fence."

The next day Donnie did indeed repair the fence. The man who owned the farm complimented Donnie about the job and said that the fence was better than it was in the beginning.

Harold says, "It should be. This is a farm boy. He knows how to put the right amount of staples in it and get the barbed wire just right."

Harold says he never actually scolded Donnie about the incident. He just pulled him out of that ditch because he figured that Donnie had already learned his lesson.

And Harold still swears today that Donnie was squeezing the girl too tight. Donnie refuted that notion and confessed. He says what actually happened is that he and his girlfriend were having a little argument and he wasn't paying attention to the road. Either way, it makes a great story for father and son to reminisce and discuss for time eternal.

Both Donnie and Dick remember Harold taking them hunting to catch rabbits for the freezer just like Harold had done with his father. They learned to hunt with beagles and they learned how to train dogs, too.

Harold recalls farmers asking him how to train their beagles to hunt. "You mean you can bark like a beagle? And that's how you train dogs?"

"Yes, I've done it for many years," Harold said.

"Well, how do you do that?"

"First, you catch a rabbit and let the dog smell around the rabbit's cage. That way the dog knows what he's after. Then you let the rabbit out of the cage. But you never shoot the rabbit. When the rabbit begins running away, I begin braying. It doesn't take long for the dogs to catch on to the idea."

If a dog couldn't be trained to bark when it was on a rabbit's trail, the Baileys called it a silencer dog. But Harold never saw a dog that he couldn't train.

Harold also taught Donnie and Dick about a 'sight chase' which is when the dog could actually see the rabbit it was chasing rather than just smelling it. A rabbit always runs in a circle so while they were training the dog, Harold and the boys would jump up onto a stump and wait. The dog would chase the rabbit right back to where they started. Then they could catch the rabbit and the dog without moving out of the original area.

Harold likes to buy the best beagles that money can buy. It's his opinion that if he buys dogs from West Virginia and Virginia they'll be better runners. He figures if they can run fast through the steep hills of those states, they can run even faster in the flat country of Ohio.

One of the neighbors, John Shuler, liked to have Harold go with him on bee tree hunts. "Hey Bailey. Let's go back and get some honey."

"Hey, I don't want to go back and get no honey. My honey's in the kitchen," laughed Harold.

After they both had a good laugh, Harold continued, "How are we gonna' do this, John?"

Whenever he was thinking, John absent-mindedly 'worked' his cigarette by chewing on the end stuck in his mouth and by moving it from side to side with his tongue as if it had a built-in motor. He formulated their plans then told Harold what he thought they should do. They would walk into the woods and look for a hollow tree. If they happened to find a hollow tree with a beehive inside, John knew there would be layers of honey cakes in the hive.

They were fortunate to find a bee tree that day. They decided to gather the honey later that night when the bees were less active and also when the moon was hidden behind clouds making the woods even darker.

John's son, Davey, pestered and begged the men until they agreed to take him. They thought it might not be a good idea to allow him to tag along but they finally gave in to his nagging. Harold hitched his John Deere tractor to John's trailer and the three of them headed for the tree.

Wiring a spotlight to the tractor's battery, they aimed it at the tree to watch what the bees were doing. When they saw that the insects had quit flying in and out of the tree for the night, they knew it was safe to harvest the golden crop that they had come there for.

Harold, after putting on gloves, reached into the tree and began removing the honeycombs. The bees had built tiers upon tiers of waxy honeycombs filled with sweet, sticky honey. He filled all of the pots and pans that they had brought with them but only as much as both families could use.

Harold's gloves became covered with bees and honey. He carefully slid them off his hands and threw them backwards away from him without looking. Unfortunately, he had forgotten that Davey was standing behind him. The gloves brushed across Davey's pants on their way to the ground leaving traces of honey stuck to his pant legs. The agitated bees frantically trying to protect their food flew off of the gloves and massed onto the honey that was clinging onto the pant material. Davey, getting stung through his pants by the retaliating bees, began yelling and running erratically into the dark.

The men couldn't see exactly where Davey had run but they could still hear him screaming. They couldn't help him as quickly as Davey would have liked because they couldn't find him at first.

"Davey learned two valuable lessons that day. Don't stand close to the man collecting the honey and when bees are stinging you, get your clothes off in a hurry instead of running," says Harold.

Harold has a theory about honey. It's not been proven by doctors but he swears it works. He says to give an older child a tablespoon of honey every night that's still in the comb, not strained, if that child is still wetting the bed and medicine doesn't help. It won't be long before that child will stay dry. He doesn't know if it will work for adults.

CHAPTER TWELVE

HIS TRAPPING PROFESSION

Trapping along with hunting was something that Harold had enjoyed doing since he was young. He had started setting traps to catch animals that were creating a nuisance when he was a young man. It was a fascination for him to capture animals that were causing problems such as destroying vegetable plants. He would then set them free in woods or open fields where they wouldn't be a bother to anyone, yet they were able to continue living a long life. Being always short of cash, he wondered if he might be able to turn one of his favorite hobbies into a lucrative business.

He began exploring the possibility of starting a trapping business. Through his investigation he learned that Ohio had a professional license called a trapper's nuisance license. He knew right then and there that this was what he needed. He had already been trapping for years so he may as well get a license and trap for profit.

Another of Harold's philosophy is that ignorance of the law is no excuse. And he wanted to be sure he was trapping within the law.

He called Dave Brown, the Mahoning County Game Protector. He thought surely Dave would know how to get the license and he was right. Not only did Dave tell him how to fulfill the requirements, he helped Harold obtain all the proper papers and licenses under state law.

His reputation as a great trapper rapidly became known throughout the community. He never had to formally advertise. Harold's accomplishments as a trapper were passed around by word of mouth. His trapping career exploded into a booming business. He soon had to purchase more and more traps because his supply could not keep up with the demand of his talent.

Harold went into AgLand, a 'good old-fashioned hardware store', in the center of Canfield to purchase supplies. He purchased all the traps that he needed for that day but Harold figured that he would soon need additional traps. He was determined to make this trapping business enlarge to a much grander scale. Being the personable, 'gabby' person that he is, he made friends with the owner and workers. He talked them into buying twenty-five additional live traps though the storeowner was wary that they would ever sell them.

Harold, in talking mostly to women, learned that they would hire him over other trappers because they didn't want any animals to get hurt. Soon, word got out that it was possible for Harold to trap an animal humanely and without too much trouble. Women would hire Harold to come catch it for them.

Eventually some people followed Harold's techniques and they purchased the live traps from AgLand to take care of the critter by themselves. And also, Harold's business required him to purchase many additional traps. AgLand began making money off of the once non-profit item and the storeowner was pleased that he needed to keep hundreds of the traps in stock.

Harold especially likes to trap groundhogs because they can do a lot of damage. The groundhogs are vegetarians. If the brown furry rodents happen to set up their homes in an alfalfa field or a cornfield, Harold says that they will strip the field bare.

Harold was puzzled at first as to where he could free groundhogs after he caught them. He soon learned that some farmers actually wanted the animals for their farms and some people actually eat them.

Harold's business grew so large that he began to resort to giving people instructions over the telephone. A young lady telephoned Harold and asked if he'd tell her how to trap a skunk.

She said, "My parents said if I trap a skunk, I'm allowed to trap this year. And I'll sell the furs to make some Christmas money."

Leary, Harold asked her, "Don't you want me to come down and show you?"

"No. I want to learn to do it by myself. Can't you just tell me over the phone?"

He told her, "Go get a live trap at AgLand's. Put an apple in the trap for bait. When the skunk gets hungry, he'll go into your trap looking for food and you'll catch him. Are you sure you don't want me to come show you?"

"Nope. I really want to do this myself."

A few days later, she called Harold frantically. "Harold, I caught the skunk. Now what am I going to do?"

"Now you've got to listen carefully to me. The first thing you got to do is to get a rug or a rag and throw it over the trap real slow. Then pick the trap up and take it back in the woods and let the skunk go."

She says she followed his directions to the letter. She picked up that skunk in the cage after throwing a blanket over it and started walking confidently through the back yard. Unfortunately as she was walking towards the back of the lot, she tripped and fell. Well, the skunk got scared and did what skunks do best. He squirted his 'lovely' scent all over her. She ran for the telephone once again.

"Harold," she cried, "now what am I gonna' do? I smell awful and I can't get the smell off of me."

"The best thing to do is to take a bath in tomato juice. Get a whole case and just pour it into the tub and soak a while."

"Harold," she called later, "I'm in trouble yet. My skin reacted to the tomato juice. I've got a rash all over and I itch like crazy. I called my doctor. He said, 'Please don't come down here, I'll call in a prescription for you'."

Harold says he never met that young lady but he did know she was a senior in high school. About three or four weeks later, he was grocery shopping in the Sparkle Market in Columbiana County. He's fairly sure that the young woman caller was on the other side of the checkout counter. He could still smell the skunk's odor in her hair.

Part of the lure of trapping for Harold was not that he actually caught an animal. The excitement was in experimenting with a bait to see which one worked the best to catch the critter he was after. He'd try various foods over and over again much like a researcher looking for the precise clues to solve a particular problem.

Sometimes, he'd meet someone who would say that there was no possible way to catch a certain animal. That only made him more determined to find a way to catch it.

An old farmer called him and said, "Boy, Harold, could you come down here? The darn fox are stealing my chickens. I see them doing it but I can't shoot my gun no more. I'm too old."

As Harold drove into the man's yard, Jake came walking out of the house. He was wearing faded bib overalls. There was drool the same color as the snuff he had tucked in his cheek dribbling out of the side of his mouth. Harold watched as he yanked a brown stained handkerchief out of his pocket, wiped the drool from his chin, and stuffed the wet hanky back into his pocket with his tobacco stained hand.

"Good morning, Jake," Harold yelled as he unloaded his truck. He pulled from the truck a piece of pipe as big around as a soccer ball, some rain gear even though it wasn't raining, Velveeta cheese, and a bottle of fox urine that he had purchased for $35.00 per bottle.

Jake had been watching him closely and said, "What are you gonna' do with that pipe?"

"I'm gonna' catch that fox."

"Well, that will never happen."

"Don't tell me it'll never happen. I do it quite often. I'm gonna' relocate this fox. That's what I'm gonna' do. Now Jake, go back inside and go to the window where you saw that fox robbing your chickens and wave at me. If I can wave at you and you can wave at me, I've got the perfect spot."

Harold put on his rain pants, his rain jacket, and gloves that reached up to his armpits so there was as little human smell in the area as possible. He dug a hole and buried the pipe in the ground at a 45-degree angle leaving the end sticking out of the ground. He put the cheese into the bottom of the pipe for bait and dripped male fox urine onto the pipe to attract the fox.

If he were lucky, the fox would be lured into the trap the same night that he had set it but Harold was willing to wait a few days before trying something different.

Harold walked back to the farmhouse and spoke to Jake, "Now I don't want anyone checking that trap but me. I'll have to be frank with you, Jake. You've got a terrible body odor and it might scare the fox. Now, I'll be by every morning to check the trap. I'll see you tomorrow."

Harold was so excited that he couldn't sleep much that night. He decided he may as well jump into his pick-up truck and head for Jake's. He had to see if anything had happened.

When he got there, Jake had the telephone in his hand getting ready to dial Harold's phone number, "Hey Harold, I was just gonna' call you. The fox is in the trap."

Harold ran to the spot carrying a potato sack. The fox had crawled into the pipe headfirst becoming stuck inside the pipe. That was exactly as Harold had planned.

He spread the potato sack "nice and flat" on the ground behind the trap. Then he took a couple of sticks and propped open the large mouth of the sack.

He could see the fox's tail sticking out of the pipe, curling upwards in a half-moon shape. Harold approached the fox confidently. The fox couldn't back up. It was stuck firmly in the pipe and it couldn't turn around so it couldn't bite him.

Harold grabbed the tail and pulled the fox out of the pipe just far enough so that he could grab onto its two back legs. He wrestled with the legs pulling the fox out of the pipe just far enough so that the legs were sticking straight out of the pipe when he held onto them. Then, in one swift motion, he pulled the fox completely out of the pipe with his right hand and stuffed him into the potato sack. Harold had a tremendous amount of power in his right hand but his left was weak as a result of a broken arm from playing sandlot football while he was still in high school. Quickly closing the sack, he tied the opening shut with bailer twine or whatever kind of rope he happened to have in his back pocket that night.

The fox was captured and the job was finished so Harold pulled the pipe out of the ground, filled the hole with dirt, and walked up to the porch to talk with Jake.

Jake asked, "Where you going with that fox, Harold?"

"I'm going down to Columbiana County and let it go."

Jake laughed and laughed at him, "It'll never happen."

"Oh yes it will. I'll have that fox loose by morning." And the fox was allowed to run to freedom through the woods in the morning just as Harold had promised.

There were times when allowing an animal to go free after trapping it wasn't in the best interests of the animal. Harold detests those occasions but it was a more humane treatment for the animal to have it destroyed.

A man telephoned Harold and said, "Harold, I need you right away. I got a coyote and it just chased my little wiener dog. That coyote is really bad."

This time, Harold decided he had to set a leg trap. He had observed the coyote before making his decision and knew that there was something wrong with its walking gait. It wasn't walking normally. Once again, he used urine to bait the trap but he used female coyote urine this time.

When he caught the coyote, he watched it again while it walked around. He says, "I looked at him and he looked at me and I could see that the back hip was badly dislocated."

There was nothing anyone could do to repair the dislocation and Harold realized that it would be cruel to turn the animal loose. It could no longer run away from its predators nor could it run fast enough to catch the food it needed to survive. Harold decided that the best thing to do was to put the animal to sleep.

Harold took the deceased animal into the woods to bury it. He dug a fairly deep hole before putting the coyote into it. He threw lime on top of the carcass to deter the growth of any harmful bacteria and then covered it with dirt.

Harold says he always disinfected his shoes after burying an animal because of the possibility of carrying germs into his home. He was always conscious of protecting any family members who liked to sit on his carpet and also his grandchildren who liked to crawl on their hands and knees while playing on the floor.

CHAPTER THIRTEEN

TRAPPING STORIES AND MORE

"I have my own way, I do my own thing, and I never keep no secrets."

Harold tells stories to anyone who will listen and he has more than one story to tell. Just get him started on the subject of trapping and he can spin yarns all day and all night. Of course, he only tells about his own personal triumphs and failures.

He's the only person he knows that can flush raccoons out of a chimney and keep them alive. Here's his technique:

He purchases an expensive flashlight "like the policemen use" costing him approximately $147.00. The more expensive flashlight gives off the most light when he's looking into a chimney. The bright light allows him to see any adult or baby raccoons that may have taken up residence even in the darkest recesses of the structure.

He secures a twenty-four to thirty-six inch long chain onto the end of a rope with duct tape. Next he tapes flares onto the chain being careful not to set the rope on fire. He makes sure that he only purchases sulphur flares because raccoons "can't handle sulphur". And the flares must be able to stay lit for at least fifteen minutes

With his equipment assembled, he begins talking to the cornered raccoon, "You're gonna' be in my cage ole' boy. Gimme five more minutes."

He then places a trap that he has designed over the top of the chimney on the roof. The trap has an opening slightly larger than twelve inches square and is made out of wire. The wire provides holes that a raccoon's claws can grasp onto thus allowing excellent footholds for the raccoon to crawl up and into the trap.

Next, he lowers the already lighted sulphur flare into the chimney allowing it to drop lower than the animal. Trapper makes sure never to burn them with the flare as he pulls the rope up slowly chasing the animal into the trap.

The animal quickly scurries up the chimney by holding onto the rope or onto the mortar between the bricks of the chimney. When the raccoon is almost out of the chimney, Trapper ducks down a little so that the animal can't see him. The raccoon climbs into the trap, Trapper shuts the lid and wires it shut.

Trapper then coos into the opening of the chimney to determine if per chance there are any babies still hiding in the chimney. Many females take their babies inside the structure for protection from the weather. If Trapper hears any cooing answering him, he knows his job isn't finished.

He goes inside to the bottom of the chimney, "I'll open up the damper real nice and slow. Ill put a mirror reflecting up at the bottom of the chimney and shine the flashlight on the mirror. That allows the light to shine up into the chimney better. I'm finally able to see in the mirror, the babies looking down at me. And I'll say 'You little fellas, you're coming with me.' I am very fortunate because lots of times I'd never wear gloves and I never got scratched. That's because I know how to handle them. I'll take the damper completely out and take out the three or four babies and put them in a cage. Now we're off to the woods. Problem solved."

In the woods, Trapper locates a hollow log lying on the ground. First, he places the babies in the log. Then he places the live trap's opening against a hole in the log, opens the lid, and allows the mother to come out. She'll sniff her babies and crawl right into the log with them. That is Trapper's clue to walk away from the reunited family. He knows they are safe and sound.

Sometimes Trapper gets called back to the same chimney to retrieve a male raccoon. He says, "After the male does his damage, the female throws him out. And he'll hit the road but they probably communicated after the babies are grown. The male will come back looking for the female because the odor will still be in the chimney. And he'll get stuck in the chimney. Then I have to go out because the people call and say 'can you help me again'?"

There are two types of chimney dampers. You use your hands on the first kind to manually turn the flap. The second one has chains and you pull a chain to open the damper's metal door. The first is the best according to Trapper. The one you open with chains is fairly good except when a raccoon lays on one of the chains and it accidentally opens. The raccoon more than likely falls into a fireplace and begins running around the living room or the bedroom. That's when Trapper gets a frantic call to come immediately.

"When I got retired and I had the time, I'd drop everything and I was on a roll. Right now! Sometimes I'd go out and bring animals in alone. When I caught the animal I'd call the people on the telephone."

Trapper likes to put wire chimney guards on all the chimneys. It keeps the wildlife from getting into the structure.

There are only a few animals that crawl into and out of a chimney on purpose, bats, raccoons, and chimney swifts. But in the winter, often birds perch on top of the chimney. When a fire is lit in a fireplace or the furnace kicks on, fumes travel up the smokestack putting the bird to sleep. It usually falls down into the chimney and if it's large enough, it becomes stuck.

Trapper declares that he's never been afraid of heights. "I've been up on every roof in downtown Youngstown. I've been on the Dollar Bank building and the five and ten cent McCrory's, well it's not a five and ten cent store any more. I don't know what's down there."

In 1987 or 1988, Ohio began experiencing a rabies outbreak with Mahoning County reporting more cases than the other 87 counties. Therefore, the state law had to be changed to protect the public from this terrible disease. Every animal that was trapped from then on had to be destroyed. They were no longer allowed to be set free.

"I didn't like it at all. I had to put everything to sleep and that was the time for me to start changing. I just didn't want to get into that."

Trapper continues, "Any time you see a fox or a skunk or a raccoon or a bat in the daylight, you have an animal that is sick, sick, sick. You cannot shoot that animal in the head. You can't freeze it. You've ruined it. (Animals are confirmed as having rabies by examining the brain tissue.) What you want to do is take the head off naturally and take it to the health department.

The last project I got into there were four rabid animals and they were all raccoons. I double bagged the animals or triple bagged them after destroying them. I'd take the head off myself. I used rubber gloves and wrap it up. The health department would come to the house and pick it up. But if I was close to them, I took it down.

Not long ago, a small child got bit out by Mosquito Lake. And that little chipmunk was rabid. The child needed to have the series of rabies shots. But they don't use the stomach any more. They give the injections in the hip or the back of the legs. I don't know how many shots they make you get and I don't know how much they cost but it is very expensive."

He resumes, "There was a tree along side of a porch and a lady was sound asleep in bed with her window up. She wasn't thinking about what was gonna' bust through that window. A raccoon jumped through that window and jumped on her bed. I caught that rabid raccoon and we sent it away to a health department.

Thank goodness we have health departments all over the country. If we didn't, we would be in big trouble. There are so many diseases.

The big health department won't allow me to go in there. I'm not afraid. I would like to know how they take these animals apart and how they know one disease from the other but I never got OK'd to go through one. I would just love to go through one. Spend the whole day."

Though trapping was his main objective, he's willing to help others with unusual problems. A man said he had a huge problem and he didn't know what to do about it. Would Harold be able to help him?

"Well, tell me about the problem and I'll see."

"I just bought an old house and there's a yellow jacket nest in there."

"That doesn't sound so bad."

"Well, you haven't seen the nest. It's got to be seven feet high and about twelve feet long."

"Now that is a problem, friend. Let's go take a look and I'll see if I can help you."

True to his word, the nest was that large. Harold had no idea how long the yellow jackets had been adding to the nest but he made sure to take a picture of it for a keepsake. He'd never seen one that big before and, frankly, he hopes he doesn't see another one like it.

In no time at all, Harold had a plan and he put it to work. He entered the building at night while properly clothed, separated the hive into manageable proportions and destroyed it.

CHAPTER FOURTEEN

ONE MORE CAREER

Working in the mill and trapping animals didn't fully satisfy the businessman inside Harold. He also longed for more money so he found another career to work into his already busy schedule. He began selling animals and transporting livestock to meat packinghouses.

Harold couldn't find a suitable truck bed that matched the image in his mind so he contacted a man in Big Bone, Kentucky.

He asked, "Could you make a truck bed to fit my specifications?"

"Well, tell me what you want. I'll think about it," said the man.

"I want a bed made with hickory and built without using any nails or screws. I don't want to scratch any animal I'd be hauling. I need you to put a floor in it halfway to the top so I can carry fifty to one hundred animals in the bottom and the same number in the top. I'd like it to be painted red to match my truck. Do you think you could make a truck bed like that?"

"Hm-m-m, that doesn't sound too hard. I think I could do that for you, Harold. When do you want it finished?"

"Well, I don't want it to take too long. How about in a month or so?" continued Harold.

"I think I can do that without much trouble. You get ready to come get it in a month, OK?"

"I'll be there."

In the meantime, Harold called a friend in Kentucky, "Can I hire you to buy two hundred and fifty goats for me? I'm comin' down there to pick up a truck bed I'm having built and I may as well pick up some goats to sell up here in the north."

When Harold arrived in Kentucky, the old bed was replaced and the new bed was attached over the rear axel behind the truck cab. He says the new bed was absolutely fantastic for him. In the meantime, the goats had been purchased and they were ready to be loaded.

The friend told Harold, "Now, I want you to go to town and have some coffee and doughnuts or something to eat and when I've got these goats loaded, I'll come to town and get you."

Harold brought the goats back to Youngstown and he sold them to people who worked in and around the mills just as he had done with his father. Many of these people were born in Puerto Rico and Harold discovered that they loved to eat goat meat. He sold the 250 goats to them rather quickly because it was just before Easter.

He says, "They ate or used just about every part of the animal. They didn't throw anything away."

Once again in his life, Harold's reliability brought him business opportunities. He'd frequently receive telephone calls asking if he'd haul animals to and from the Youngstown area. While he was working afternoon turn at the mill, he eventually made a permanent schedule to deliver the goats and cattle. He visited every sale barn around the Youngstown area. On Monday, he hauled animals to and from New Wilmington, Pennsylvania and Carrollton, Ohio. Tuesday was the day he headed for Damascus, Ohio and on Wednesday, he stayed in and around Canfield. On Thursdays, he traveled to Bloomfield or Kidron, Ohio and on Friday, he headed to Scio. He finished out the week on Saturday by traveling to Barnesville. After he finished taking the animals to where they needed to be hauled on that particular day, he'd head for the mill to work his shift.

When Harold was called to go down to Scio, Ohio, he'd be hired to haul an entire load of steer to Chardon, Ohio. He'd leave early in the morning and the farmers would have the steer prepared to be loaded. The steer would be fed and watered and waiting in pens. They then could be loaded onto the truck bed within a short period of time.

Harold says that the farmers were very generous to him. They'd tell him to make sure he was in their area at breakfast or dinnertime. He'd call them prior to leaving to tell them what time he would arrive at their farm.

Harold's experiences with rheumatic fever and the health habits he developed after he became well continued into his adult life. If he had to use a public telephone to make his phone calls, he carried rubbing alcohol with him. He correctly assumed that the receiver of a telephone is a great place for bacteria and other germs to grow. He'd use the alcohol to remove as many germs as possible from the receiver before using the telephone. He attributes this practice to helping him stay well.

The farmers would ask, "How many eggs do you want?"

Harold replied with a question, "What kind of eggs do you have? You know I don't dirty my mouth for just one egg."

They'd joke with him, "White."

"Now-w-w, what kind of eggs do you have? How heavy are they?" Harold used to know by looking at the eggs approximately what the eggs weighed. He wouldn't want just one or two of the pullet eggs, the first eggs a chicken laid and they were always the smallest. He'd want three or four of 'them fellas'.

Harold would pull into the barnyard and smell the fresh homemade bacon or sausage cooking on the grill. The farmers and he would eat a great big meal and carry on a lengthy conversation before he unloaded the steer and before he headed for home.

" I remember once we had to load a semi truck with hogs. We had to go way down into Pennsylvania and Maryland when it was seventy-five degrees. And what did we do? We went down to the icehouse and purchased blocks of ice. We placed it in the top deck. The hogs in the upper deck, and there might have been a hundred of them, remained cool from the frozen ice and when the ice melted, it dripped onto the hogs below allowing them to keep cool.

I also remember hauling hogs in the wintertime. And we had our problems again. One time we had to go over to Somerset, Pennsylvania and we still had the slots in the truck. The hogs were frozen stiff by the time we got to the packinghouse."

He was thrilled that the butchers had so much faith in him. It got to the point where some of the butchers in the area began asking, "Hey, Mr. Bailey, do you know of anywhere to get some good lambs? Like twenty-five of them?"

"Yeah. I know where I can get them." To keep their confidence, he always took his time to pick the choicest lambs from a farmer. The packers would pay him to deliver the lambs to a specific destination.

To make the process smoother and quicker, Harold would call a certain farmer and say, "Hey, would you separate your lambs from their mothers? I need twenty-five super good lambs today. You set your price and I want to 'back' them."

Harold says, "I'd take my hand and back the lamb and that always told me where the good lamb was at. That means I'd take my hand and feel back by the hips. If I could feel a good back, solid and firm, I got a good lamb. The next thing I'd do was to look in the lamb's mouth. If it had baby teeth, it was a baby lamb."

Harold remembers delivering one or two hundred lambs to Pittsburgh more than once. His customer would have a barbecue pit filled with hot coals ready to cook the animals. People stood in line to purchase the meat and the man charged an additional twenty-five cents for the head. The head was considered a delicacy because the sweetest meat on the animal was located there.

He recalls going to Pittsburgh one snowy day. Harold told the man, "I don't know if I can make it up your road. It's too slippery."

The customer said, "Where are you? I'll have a slag truck down there right away to meet you." And the entire driveway was scattered with slag so Harold could drive up to the top of the mountain.

Harold says he discovered by trial and error a special gift that he had. He began performing veterinary type of work. He never opened a formal textbook. The ideas just came to his mind and he knew what he should be doing to correct a problem.

He says, "I cured some animals that veterinarians couldn't and I did it in my own way. My treatments were by guess and by garwsh and the animal would get better."

One trick he learned was when tears were running down a steer's or a cow's face, chances were good that the animal had pinkeye. Pinkeye could pose a serious danger to the animal. It was possible that it could go blind if the infection wasn't treated.

"There was no use fighting with the cow. I'd just put salt brine in a sprayer bottle similar to the sprayers women used to wash windows. I adjusted the sprayer to shoot a steady stream of brine instead of a fine spray. Then I'd walk up to the cow and squirt a stream of the saltwater into its eye. It would clean out the stuff known as pinkeye. The eye usually healed within two days and the brine saved the sight of the animal," says Harold.

John from next door called him, "Hey, Bailey, I need some help right away. I got a cow with an apple stuck in its throat."

"Where's the cow at?"

"She's out in the pasture."

"Get that cow in a stanchion—quickly. I'll be right over."

John was waiting for Harold when he drove into the driveway. Harold yelled, "Go get the garden hose. Your cow is choking. You're gonna' lose this cow."

Harold made sure that the hose had a metal gasket on one end. Then he shoved the hose down the cow's throat hitting the apple with the gasket. The gasket drove the apple into the cow's second stomach thus saving the cow's life.

"Now people don't know you can do that. And when I see an apple tree in a field, I am concerned about that. Because at that time, that guy called three veterinarians and they couldn't come. Today, you have a telephone and they can get there immediately."

Licensed veterinarians did threaten to report him to state authorities. Two came onto his front porch and called him out of the house. "Bailey, you'd better quit saying you're a veterinarian. You haven't got a license to practice this kind of medicine and it's against the law."

"Well fellas, I'm not promoting myself as a veterinarian. And I'm not practicing medicine because I never charge one red cent for the work I do. So why'd you want to be bothering me? I'm not gonna' quit because these farmers are so garwsh darned poor. They're as poor as a church mouse and I'm gonna' help them whenever they ask me."

"Well, we'll be watching you," they warned.

"That's OK. If you get in trouble and I can help you, feel free to call me. I do stuff different than you guys do, I'll guarantee that."

And he did guarantee his work. He eventually did have some veterinarians call him for problems that they couldn't solve.

CHAPTEN FIFTEEN

KAREN'S RECOLLECTIONS

Harold and a car salesman stopped at a small diner to have a cup of coffee. Not only did they enjoy the coffee but it also proved fruitful for Harold's stepson, Dick. Waiting on their table was a lovely young girl named Karen.

Karen had been Harold's waitress a few other times so Harold struck up a conversation with her, "Do you like to write to guys in Viet Nam?"

"Well, I guess I do. Do you have someone in mind?"

"You bet I do. If you're willing to give me your name and address, I'll send it to my stepson. He's a great guy and you won't be sorry."

Karen really doesn't know why she trusted Harold but she did. She liked him from the moment she had first seen him. She decided that it would be safe to give him her name and address. It was important for her to support our men who were fighting for our country. After all, what harm could there be in writing to a lonely soldier that needed mail in a far away country.

She had written to Dick for approximately five months when, out of the blue, Harold called her, "Hey, Karen. Dick is coming home tomorrow and I want to know if you'd like to go to the airport with us to pick him up?"

"You bet. I'd like to meet this guy I've been writing to."

Harold proved to be a good matchmaker. Karen and Dick dated for five years and, after that, they were married. They had two children, little Richie and Tara.

Karen recalls that she found out the hard way about Harold being a practical joker. While Karen and Dick were dating, Harold and Dick convinced her to go with them on a snipe hunt. Falling for the joke 'hook, line, and sinker' as the saying goes, Karen was convinced that they were going to take her to look for a type of fish. It took a long time for her to figure out that there never was a kind of fish called snipe. By the time they got home, she was exhausted and had mosquito bites all over her arms and legs. All three of them still laugh about the incident and, at times, the two men kid with Karen by asking if she has seen any snipes lately.

Karen adores Harold. Her father had passed away so she adopted Harold to take the job. She thinks he's a very wise man. She can confide in him and tell him anything on her mind. She laughed because she has even been known to "tell him off" a time or two and they remain as close as any father and daughter.

She's never heard Harold say anything bad about anyone no matter if he cares for the person or not.

But he always says what he thinks. She's heard him be blunt when speaking to a person at times but even if what he says hurts a little, it's always true. She's adamant that he doesn't tell fibs.

Karen, a school teacher at South Range Schools for thirty years, helped to change his opinion on a few issues or so she believes. When she first met Harold, his attitude towards education tended to be a little on the negative side. He used to tell her that a formal education from books wasn't all that important and he's proven it because he's a self-made man. He believed that teachers were paid too much money and that they should only be a teacher if they loved the profession. It shouldn't matter how much they were getting paid. After her goading, she thinks she played a part in convincing him that it was important to vote for the school levies so that all the children could have the best education possible from the best teachers possible.

Karen and Dick built a house and moved onto some of the acreage that belonged to Harold and Elsie. A wooded lot separated the two properties with a small creek running through the woods. A small plank bridge was built over the creek so that the two families could visit one another without walking on the road. Not only did they share land, the two families also liked to do many things together.

Karen liked to accompany Harold when he went to deliver the livestock. She enjoyed spending the day with him and oftentimes all they accomplished was talking.

One trip, however, didn't turn out quite as they expected. Harold had taken her to a livestock auction. They were sitting in the middle of the crowd "talking up a storm" to each other. The conversation became so engrossing that neither one of them were paying attention to what was happening around them. Karen began using her hands to emphatically make a point. The auctioneer, seeing her hand waving in the air, mistook her gesture for a bid. Unintentionally, Karen had bought a cow. Karen always tried to sit on her hands after that incident when she went to auctions with Harold.

Karen suspects that Harold secretly yearned to become an auctioneer. She confessed that many times she had heard Harold standing in the wooded lot that separated them. She couldn't see him but she heard the rhythm of auctioneer chatter emitting from the trees in his voice. She suspects that he longed to go to school to learn the trade but that was one thing he never did.

Harold's job at the mill ended in 1987 with the closing of the Youngstown Sheet and Tube, as did many steel mills in Youngstown. They lost their business to mills around the world and it began a black era in Youngstown history. Many men lost their jobs and the economic levels in all of Mahoning County dropped.

Harold was at a loss for a while wondering what his future held but he never went for want of something to do. Harold would get up in the morning, traipse over to Karen and Dick's and say, "What are we gonna' do with the kids today?" Karen would know who was at the door before his familiar knock sounded because she would see the top of his hat pass in front of their windows.

Harold helped Dick build a tree house for his grandchildren. It was important to both men to include the children in its construction. The kids would climb into the tree and pound nails into boards while standing alongside Harold and their father. The building of the house taught them lessons in building structures and how to be good parents with the examples set by Harold and Dick.

Karen recalls one time when Tara wasn't very old; the men were building a pole barn. Karen looked out the window and saw Tara up on the roof of the barn with them. It was terrifying to watch because Tara only had her summer thongs on her feet. Thongs are basically a rubber sole with two rubber straps shaped in a V. The point of the V pokes through the sole in-between the spot a person places his/her first and second toes. The "point" pulled out of the sole frequently whenever a person walked.

Little Richie was privy to one of his grandfather's practical jokes one evening after dark. Harold swears that it didn't start out to be a practical joke but it ended up that way.

Harold told him, "Come on, little Richie. Let's build a kite and I'll show you how to fly it."

They built the kite together making it out of newspaper and sticks. They painted the kite jet black and tied a small penlight the size of a man's finger onto its rag tail. They painted a thin coat of red fingernail polish over the entire flashlight bulb.

Harold took little Richie out to their field later that night to show him how to fly the kite. After launching it, it sailed so high into the sky that the only thing the two could see was the red light floating back and forth like an apparition, a ghost.

Before long, the perfectly innocent pair noticed five cars stopped alongside the road. They realized that the occupants were trying to figure out what was the unidentified flying object .

Harold and little Richie laughed until they snorted through their noses but they stayed hidden in the weeds. They decided not to reveal their secret to the occupants of the cars.

After sixteen years, Dick and Karen's marriage came to an end. It was difficult for Harold and Elsie to accept the fact that the couple no longer wanted to be married. She's not sure that Trapper remembered the famous saying adopted from his father, every new broom sweeps clean. Karen still isn't positive if they ever came to terms with it.

Today, Karen and Dick are both married to other spouses but Karen's relationship with Harold has never changed. She continues to love him dearly.

CHAPTER SIXTEEN

HIS 4-H PASSION

"I love 4-H children. They do not get enough credit in this world. I've only seen a couple of 4-H children go wrong in my lifetime."

Harold's passion for children involved in the 4-H program runs deep within his soul. He is convinced that every child should become involved with this organization, which teaches children how to farm and to raise animals because it is such an excellent program. His passion began about thirty years ago when he was selling livestock to packinghouses.

"What I like about 4-H is that most of the children in Mahoning County get to keep the money for the animals that they raise and sell. The parents initially invest the money to buy the steer or the animal but the children have to care for them. They have to brush them, feed them, water them, and they have to exercise them. And I know a young lady who put herself through college by selling her steer because the parents allowed her to have all the money."

Harold goes out of his way to help the organization by promoting the sale of animals raised by 4-H'ers. He's been known to knock on meatpackers' doors and inform the packers about a sale that would be coming up. He also likes to cajole people into buying the animals.

He remembers talking to Bob Lloyd, "Bob, come on up to the sale and buy yourself some steer or buy yourself some hogs or buy a lamb or two. Then the next year, you'll get your tickets free."

"I don't know if I want to go up there to the sale or not. I'll think about it."

"If you buy the animals, you can write it off on income tax because the money is going to a charity. You get ahold of your accountant and look into it."

Bob's accountant must have agreed with Harold because that night Bob did go to the sale and he purchased some animals. Harold guesses he spent between three and four thousand dollars.

Harold saw people bring orders for others to 4-H sales. They came to the sales and picked the steers based on the quality of their hides. The people would then sell the meat and the hides separately. If they could sell the hides of at least ten steers, which could be worth $5.00 apiece, the fifty dollars from the hides would pay for their truck expenses.

Harold recalls a man who sold automobiles in Youngstown on Market St. He tried to convince the man to come to a 4-H sale. "Hey, why don't you come out and buy a couple of steers? You could advertise that people could come in, buy a new Chrysler and you'd serve them a sit-down dinner."

"Ahhh Bailey, I don't know if I want to do that or not."

"I'll have you on TV," coaxed Harold.

"You know I have stock in that one TV station in town. I can be on any time I want."

"Good, then you already have an in. Here are six tickets. Please come to the sale."

Harold thought he'd probably run into the one man that he couldn't persuade. Then to Harold's surprise, the man came to the auction and sat beside him.

The auction continued on and on but the man wasn't bidding on anything. Harold turned to him and said, "Why don't you buy one of those Grand Champion's? You'll get your picture in the paper."

"If I want to be in the newspaper or on TV, I'll advertise on my own."

With those words, Harold was finally convinced that he hadn't succeeded in selling this man on the benefits of purchasing the 4-H animals. He was so disappointed.

Then lo and behold, the man began bidding. By the time the auction ended, he had purchased six steers and some lambs.

The man must have liked the animals because he returned the following year to purchase dairy cattle for his farm. And if he couldn't attend the sales, he'd ask Harold to purchase livestock for him.

"There's a definite difference in 4-H steers," Harold explains. "They're graded and sometimes the best one doesn't win the prize. There's only one Grand Champion and only one Reserved Champion at a fair. Some of the families have entered their cattle as many times as five years in a row and have never been awarded that honor."

When Harold was selling meat to the packinghouses, he found that the packers would pay extra money to him if he purchased animals raised by a 4-H child. Harold said the reason a packer could afford to throw in a few extra dollars for him was that there were two ways to purchase an animal. When a farmer kept the animal from drinking and eating the night before it was purchased, there was three percent shrinkage in the animal's total weight. The second way was to allow the animal to continue to eat and drink but to subtract three percent from the animal's total weight when it was sold. These methods of selling assured a packer that the seller was weighing mostly meat and not the water that would be stored in the meat. Harold says that the latter is still the way it's done at county fairs.

Harold began roaming from county fair to county fair purchasing the best 4-H animals that he could. Soon, the continuous traveling in addition to working at the mill proved to be too taxing on him. He became exhausted and he knew that he wasn't spending as much time with his family as he should. He finally conceded that something had to change. He had to decide what was more important; earning the extra money or being a bigger part of his family's life. He made the decision to only purchase animals from within Mahoning County. He would be close to home and he could continue to pursue an interest that he enjoyed.

His decision led him to become unhappy within himself. He wasn't helping the organization as much as he wanted, so he thought about finding another way he could help the children without running from county to county to purchase animals. He spoke to Ralph, the man who was in charge of the 4-H organization in Mahoning County. He proposed a project for the children that didn't involve agriculture.

"Ralph, I want the 4-H children to be shown what it's like to get into trouble. How about if we take them to the courthouse and let them sit in the jury box one day and watch the court proceedings? And I want them to pay attention and if they don't, I'm gonna' go tell them about it."

Ralph thought it was a great idea so he asked Harold to make the arrangements.

Harold went to the Mahoning County Courthouse and talked to a judge. He said, "Judge, I want to bring the 4-H children in here and let them sit in the jury box. Is that agreeable with you?"

The judge looked at the court docket and said, "That's fine. We don't have a jury seated on Wednesday. Can you bring them in then?"

"I think that can be arranged. I'll call Ralph and tell him."

The judge said, "Harold, I think this is a fine idea. It's wonderful to educate children in this manner."

The impact on the children from observing court proceedings has helped many young adults scrutinize the consequences of their actions. They have witnessed prisoners being brought into a courtroom and know why the prisoners have been arrested. They have heard the judge pronounce sentence upon the prisoners such as taking away their driving privileges or sending the prisoner to jail.

He cited one example in particular that moved the children emotionally. A young lady was brought into the courtroom wearing handcuffs and leg shackles. There were tears running down her mother's cheeks. It was clear to everyone that both the lady and the mother were feeling totally disgraced.

Harold firmly believes that every child in school should witness first-hand how our county court systems operate. "It's very educational and it's a lesson that can't be learned in books."

Many years after taking 4-Her's to one of these sessions, Harold met a woman in the farm bureau parking lot. She said to him, "My son wants to see you. He's waiting in my car. Would you mind going over to him?"

The young man looked up at Harold and said, "Trapper, you stopped me from getting arrested. I listened to you. I listened to the judge. I was gonna' do some bad things out there but it never happened. Thank you."

CHAPTER SEVENTEEN

RADIO AND TELEVISION BEGIN

Iva Kearns' cat brought her the present from outdoors. But the chipmunk that was now running loose in the kitchen and hiding in the back of the stove was calamitous to Iva. She couldn't cook, she was afraid to go into the kitchen, and she couldn't chase the darn chipmunk back outside. The woman called Harold for help.

Harold looked over the situation and decided that the first thing he needed to do was to make a live trap out of a coffee can. He devised it so that when the chipmunk ran into the can, the lid fell down trapping him inside.

When the trap was set, Harold asked, "Would you mind putting your cat out until we catch this thing? It will never come out if the cat's in here. A chippy is afraid of cats and yours will only scare it into hiding on us. Or if your cat finds its hiding spot, he'll just bring the chippy to you again to show you what a beautiful job he did."

"Heavens no. I don't mind. Just catch that animal before it does any damage in here."

Iva called in the morning, "Hey, Mr. Bailey, I caught that chippy! I've put it on the front porch."

"You caught it already? Well, that's just great. I'll be up there soon and take care of it."

Harold hopped into his car and drove to the woman's house. He took the caged chipmunk out to the woods and let the chipmunk go. Before he released the chippy, he warned him, "You've got to hide to stay alive little fella'." He always talks to his animals before he releases them.

Harold says that sometimes nature stories can be gross but it's just nature. He especially warned this little guy because a chipmunk is a meal for the hawk, the gray fox, the red fox, and the owls. If the chipmunk happened to run out into an open area and a hawk spotted him, that hawk could swoop down at ninety miles an hour and grab him for dinner. A hawk can render a chipmunk unconscious by hitting it with his wings because the wings are long and powerful. It's possible that a hawk would only " knock the wind out of him". But either way, the chipmunk would not be able to defend itself. A hawk then holds a chipmunk in its claws and flies up into a tree. It perches there to eat the small rodent possibly saving some part for breakfast.

Mrs. Kearns was so grateful that she steadfastly told Harold, "Mr. Bailey, you should go ahead and get in touch with Vince Camp at WBBW. You know so many things that would help a lot of people. People would think the world of you because you're so down to earth."

"I think that's a pretty good idea, Mrs. Kearns, a darn good idea, Iva."

Not waiting for Harold to take the initiative, Iva Kearns took matters into her own hands. She called Vince Camp and made an appointment for Harold to go see him.

Harold drove to the radio station with all of his live traps in tow. He waited for Vince Camp to come into his office. Mr. Camp came in a little late that day and he didn't have time to talk with Harold. Harold thought surely he had been given the brush-off. But then Harold was told that he'd be called later that evening at home.

Not only did a professional relationship begin that fateful night but a warm lifelong friendship developed also.

Harold reminisces:

"What a program that was! Vince Camp was my emcee and it was one of the hottest things that ever happened to Mahoning County. That's how I got my nickname. Vince gave it to me...the Friendly Trapper not only because I chuckled a lot but also because I was a friend to a lot of people.

I don't know a person out there that doesn't like me. I'm sure there are, I'm not a privileged character. But so many times I walk up to a person and jokingly say, 'Hey you, I'm looking for a person that doesn't like me.' And that brings out a laugh like you never believe. But no one's ever said that they didn't like me.

However, every time you get new people in, it changes things. Every new broom sweeps clean. So I was out the door. I honestly don't remember how long I worked for that station but I enjoyed it immensely. I helped thousands and thousands of people on WBBW as the Friendly Trapper. People still come up to me today and say, 'that was a great show at WBBW'.

Vince finally lost his job, too. He was eventually rehired but it's called something else now."

Harold wasn't out of the broadcasting business for very long. WYTV television, channel 33 in Youngstown contracted with Trapper to have his first television show. He appeared on '11:30 Live'. His show's format was to demonstrate his contraptions. He showed some of the traps that he made and told how to get rid of pests. His popularity gained by leaps and bounds.

Nonetheless, he says, "every new broom sweeps clean and I was out of there."

Then a representative of WKBN radio contacted him and asked if he would come to their station for a meeting with Dan Rivers and Bill Kelley.

The manager asked, "Are you doing anything with a radio station now?"

"No."

"Do you have any contracts signed with anyone?"

"Well, no I don't."

"We'd like to try you out on WKBN. We'd title your show 'The Friendly Trapper.' We don't know if the show will be continued but we'd like to try it."

"Hm-m, that sounds just fine. When do I start? I can carry two hours with no sweat."

"We're thinking that the show could be expanded to two hours eventually but, for right now, we're only willing to start with an hour program."

"Well, that's OK. I'm sure that my show will boost your ratings up and we're gonna' get people calling in here and wanting to go longer than one hour." And that's exactly what took place.

Ron Verb was the first emcee to invite Harold onto his radio program. Harold once again was an instant success with the public.

Pete Gabriel is the emcee for Trapper's current WKBN radio show. The ratings for the show skyrocketed from the beginning and Harold's ratings remain high today even though his program is currently broadcast at 6:00 in the morning. It is even said that his show is one of the most powerful shows in the entire Mahoning Valley.

He enjoys laughing and "cutting up" a little on the program. He jokes with Pete Gabriel and his callers as if he were sitting around your dining room table sharing a cup of coffee.

Trapper loves to share stories on the air about his personal life and the exciting happenings for he and Marie during the week previous to his Saturday morning program. The audience can then become familiar with his private life. This format lends itself to making the audience feel that Trapper is one of their best friends and I can assure you he truly feels that way.

A favorite story from his radio career is about a lady listener calling him one morning to tell him how much she liked his radio program. She said, "Trapper, I listen to you every Saturday. Now, I have six children and a husband and I don't want to wake them up. So, I take my radio and place it under the bed covers so I can listen to you without disturbing them. I tell everyone that it's just you and me, honey, under the covers."

"I feel real proud when I leave that radio station. I feel that I've honestly accomplished something," says Trapper.

Harold was then asked to do some television spots on WKBN TV with Rich Morgan. Viewers can always tell that they enjoy working together by watching their interaction with each other.

Harold says that Rich will call him and say, "What do you want to do today? I've got the morning free, Trapper." Oftentimes, Rich will call him more than once during a week.

"OK. I'm free, too. Let's do something." And Trapper will take Rich Morgan out to a site to film a segment. Oftentimes they will arrive unannounced to the owner. Trapper says that he knows of no one who has ever been offended by him just showing up on their doorstep. They seem excited when he comes into their store or onto their farm.

Sometimes, Trapper will opt to demonstrate something in the studio instead of taking Rich out to a different location. He loves to show how to sprout trees in the refrigerator in the winter. He places peat moss in a jar, dampens it, and places nuts on top of the moss. He might choose walnuts or acorns or any kind of nut that one finds on Ohio's trees. He punches many holes in the lid of the jar so that air can circulate in and out of it. He then tells you to place the jar in the back of your refrigerator and forget about it until spring. Around April, if the meats of the nuts were 'good', the nuts will have sprouts on them.

People have called him and said, "Trapper, I forgot about that jar. I happened to look in the back of my refrigerator the other day and the tree's growing clear out of the top of the lid out of those holes."

This segment has been repeated more than once on television because viewers have requested it.

CHAPTER EIGHTTEEN

HIS PROFESSIONAL CAREER ESCALATES

"I really don't like to call what I do a career. I just have so darn much fun!"

Trapper's success on the radio broadcasts led to an explosion in his professional career. He had only been on the air a short time when invitations to come speak to several organizations were extended.

His first speaking engagement was for the American Association of Retired Person's Organization. AARP members loved the man who was down to earth and gave solutions that were affordable.

It didn't take long for other organizations to contact him. He has spoken before Boy Scout functions, in public libraries, at Grange meetings, and before many other organizations too numerous to mention.

Trapper now averages forty to fifty speaking engagements per year. That may not sound like an extraordinary amount until one thinks about it. This is a man past seventy years old who continues to broadcast on several weekly radio stations and to appear on television almost every Monday morning.

His speaking engagements average one speech a week in addition to his regular work and he also manages to squeeze vacations into his free time.

Being on the lecture circuit is rejuvenating for him. He loves meeting all the people and sharing his knowledge with them. He especially likes being asked for a return engagement the following year. He talks to the people who attended his presentation the previous year and asks if his solutions really worked. He wants to know for example if his solution for killing ants has succeeded and if "they aren't dead or belly-up", he wants to know that, too. He more than likely has already worked on a new solution to try.

Harold always wants his experiments to work without using any chemicals. He wants to be able to use only natural and environmentally safe products to fix a problem although that isn't always possible.

He recalls speaking to a group of 115 Boy Scouts. The scoutmaster approached him after his talk and said, "Boy, Trapper, this is the quietest these boys have ever been."

Occasionally, he'd meet one of the scouts while out and about in the neighborhood. They invariably would say, "Trapper, I had a lot of fun the other night."

Trapper would ask him, "And just what did you do, you turkey?" He called the children "turkeys" when he was especially fond of them.

"I made my own kite just like you did for your grandson. And I sprayed it all black and I got myself a little flashlight and then I used my mother's fingernail polish and I painted the bulb red. I flew it at night just like you did."

"And did you see the red light up in the sky when you flew it?"

"I sure did. It was neat!"

The scout also remembered Trapper saying that it wasn't necessary to pour gasoline in a hole to kill yellow jackets that have made a nest in the ground.

"I told my father to pour scalding hot water into the hole instead. We waited until after 10 o'clock at night when it was dark just like you told us to. We didn't even get stung and we didn't have to use any gasoline to get rid of them."

Trapper spoke to the group of scouts on more than one occasion. Once, he took a part of a beaver to a meeting. He had found the animal dead on the highway, probably the result of a car hitting it as it crossed the road. He had mounted the beaver's skin onto a board and stood it up by the wall for all the boys to see. The boys measured themselves beside the skin and were amazed that the beaver was taller than them.

Some of the scouts from that group still seek out Trapper to this day to talk to him. They are now around eighteen or nineteen years old and some of them are married.

Trapper recalls an occasion when politicians came to his speaking engagement. They hadn't come to listen to him but to do some political campaigning since there were a large number of people gathered together in one hall.

Trapper says the man in charge politely told them, "Trapper is speaking. You are welcome to stay and listen to him but please don't do any campaigning." The politicians thanked the man and walked out.

One of Trapper's proudest memories of a speaking engagement was at Northside Hospital in Youngstown. He was asked to speak to the nurses about bats and raccoons and the appearance of their bite marks.

He says, "I told them I'd be glad to come to talk to everyone. But please just reserve me a place to park my car." The employees gladly gave him a special spot by the emergency room and he walked from there to a conference room.

There were so many employees wanting to listen to what he had to say that they spilled outside the room and into the hallway. He said the average age of the staff was young so they were unfamiliar with how the bite marks looked and how much damage the animals could do.

Doctors continue to call on Trapper with special requests to this day. He's been invited to banquets to speak before 100-200 people.

As Trapper's fame grew, other radio stations began asking Trapper if he would broadcast a show for them. Some of the programs could be aired from his home. He would talk on the telephone to the station and the show was transmitted over the airways through the studio.

A list of radio talk shows he has either performed for in the past or is currently appearing on are: WOHI in East Liverpool, Ohio, KMOG Radio in Payson, Arizona, WPIC in Sharon, Pennsylvania, WMAN Radio in Mansfield, Ohio, and KDKA in Pittsburgh, Pennsylvania, and WCCO in Minneapolis, Minnesota. Other states that he has broadcast in are Florida, West Virginia, Nevada, Tennessee, and both of the Carolinas. He's also done a radio show in Canada.

Soon, Trapper was asked to put his solutions into print. He has written several articles for the Farm Show paper, a publication for the agricultural community that has a circulation of approximately 146,000 newspapers. He receives many letters from readers who want him to write articles on a regular basis. They beg for pictures to be printed with the articles or to have a picture sent directly to the letter writer.

He's also written articles for the Farm and Dairy paper. That newspaper advertises about farm equipment auctions and other items of interest for farmers. Included within the magazine is a networking article of sorts where readers can ask for information such as an old recipe that they can't find anywhere. They usually get a response from someone who knows the answer.

Trapper mania grew in Minnesota unbeknownst to him simply by writing articles for these agricultural papers. Denny Long from WCCO contacted Trapper to see if he would broadcast a show with him. Denny's show was aired on Saturday. Trapper thought it was a great idea and he agreed to air it from his home but he really would like to do the show from the studio rather than over the telephone.

Trapper says, "Denny always allows me to finish my story."

Anyone talking to Trapper knows he tends to ramble a little. He likes it that Denny doesn't cut his conversation short. He can take the time to solve a person's problem thoroughly before proceeding to the next caller.

Trapper went to a Pennsylvania store for a marketing promotion. He looked at a bin of watermelons sitting in the store noting that the storeowner was charging $3.00 per melon. He considered the price to be a bargain but customers were passing them by. Trapper was told that the manager didn't know what else he should do to sell the melons before they spoiled.

On discovering the manager's dilemma, Trapper said to him, "Come on out here a minute, friend. Do you want me to sell the melons in that bin?"

"Sure. But how are you going to do that?"

"I'll tell you how. You go back in the store and get me an old-fashioned broom bristle. Like the ones from the brooms that the blind people make. I want a straw broom bristle. When you lay a watermelon on a table and you put that bristle on the top, that bristle will roll over if the melon's ripe. Guaranteed."

The manager did as Trapper requested. The straw was placed on the watermelon but it didn't do anything. They watched as the bristle continued to lie still on the fruit.

The manager said, "I'm not sure you know what you're talking about."

"Yes, I do. You didn't see the straw roll over, did you? Well, let's take this watermelon in the back room and slice it and I'll explain to you what's wrong."

Lo and behold, the meat of the watermelon was white when they sliced it open. It wasn't ripe, just as Trapper had predicted.

Going back outside to continue with the marketing of his book, a woman recognizing him came up to him and said, "Hi, Trapper. What are you doing here today?"

"I'm gonna' pick you out a nice watermelon, honey. If I can find you a ripe one, will you buy it? I'll guarantee it by putting this broom straw on it."

"Oh, I don't know Trapper. I'll just cut a plug in it."

"Honestly, you don't need to plug it. I want you to be surprised when you get home." Trapper put that broom bristle on it and the bristle went crazy, spinning around and around.

He sold the entire bin of watermelons by using only a couple of broom bristles and a little persuasion.

Trapper says, "I wonder why they always cut a plug with three sides? They never cut it any other shape. Maybe it's better eating that way?"

Trapper has also been chosen by the Udder Cream Company to be its representative. The product, which is to be used as an all-over body lotion, is manufactured in Salem, Ohio. Trapper really loves the product so he says Bill Kennedy Sr. chose him because he knew Trapper didn't have to exaggerate about how good the cream really is.

"Bill Kennedy is the kind of guy I love. I sit right along side him and we chew the fat."

Trapper uses Udder Cream regularly and even has a solution for the aches and pains of arthritis using the product. He says, "All you have to do is to stir in about five aspirins with the cream and smooth it onto what hurts."

CHAPTER NINETEEN

CLOWNING AROUND

Being a practical joker, adoring children, and enjoying the spotlight led Harold to an organization that blended all three of those loves into one big happy ball. What else could fulfill those requirements any better? He became a clown!

Trapper became a member of the Aut Mori Grotto lodge as soon as he was first invited to join. His main intention was to be voted into the clown unit and the men thought he would be a natural for the part. The only other things that Harold needed to become a successful clown were an outfit, a clown name and a clown face.

He asked his fellow lodge members if his clown name could reflect his career. The lodge voted on this idea. They unanimously agreed that he would always be known as the Friendly Trapper whether on radio, on television, or when he was just clowning around. The men decided that his clown face should resemble that of a raccoon. But Trapper prefers not to wear any makeup.

Jean Pitts, having known Trapper prior to joining, gave him the clown suit that had belonged to her husband. Trapper wears the suit with honor. You'll see him sporting the red plaid jacket with red and green lapels whenever he transforms into Trapper the clown. The jacket is worn over a white shirt and a wide red tie dotted with white polka dots. The outfit is further customized with his trademark, the white floppy hat.

The Aut Mori Grotto lodge is known around the United States for their clown units and for doing charitable work for children. The clowns give performances for institutions as well as individuals. The Grotto clowns are known for helping children by cheering pediatric patients in hospitals. They also march in numerous parades. Some units have special vehicles that the clowns can drive instead of walking the entire parade route. The vehicles are decorated to look like trolley cars or miniature old-fashioned automobiles or like any other festive vehicle that can hold several men. The clowns jump in and out of the vehicles handing candy to children along the parade route. They also bend balloons into different shapes and cartoon characters for them. Some men can turn the long slender balloons into dogs or cats or they can fold them into the shape of a heart. The Grotto holds a circus every year in Youngstown and asks people to sponsor children so that the underprivileged can attend without paying admission.

All of their performances are voluntary. They never charge for them but, of course, donations are gladly accepted. The donations help the men purchase balloons by the thousands. They also help defer the costs of transporting the clowns to and from their performances. And donations also help the men buy the special makeup and outfits that the clowns wear.

Trapper says, "You're known by the company that you keep and all these men are terrific. They always seem happy and anyone who sees a performance by the Grotto clowns can see that they enjoy what they're doing.

Some of them are getting up in age now and, for some reason, the younger generation isn't taking ahold and that's bad. We need the younger generation to get in there and help.

It's a lot of fun. When you get a carload of clowns going some place, you're almost tired when you get there because you're laughing all the way."

CHAPTER TWENTY

HIS KNOWLEDGE GOES TO PRINT

After ending his talk with the fifteen ladies from the Youngstown Garden Club, Mrs. Brayer suggested, "You know, Mr. Bailey, you should write a book. You have a lot of knowledge and you use a lot of different ways to get rid of pests without using chemicals. I'll bet that a lot of people would like to know how to do that. And I wouldn't be surprised if it would be the only kind of book like it in the entire country."

"Hm-m-m. That does sound like a good idea but I don't know how to write a book."

"Well, I think I know just the person to help you out. My husband, Ken, is in that kind of business and he'll know what you should do."

Trapper transforming into author was something he never envisioned in his entire life. He never liked school. He didn't particularly like to read. But once again, the thought of helping multitudes of people tugged at his heartstrings.

He began writing his first book in 1987 under the direction of Ken Brayer. It didn't contain many pages when it was first published but it has grown to more than double its original size over the years. The book did become a big hit just as Mrs. Brayer had predicted. Trapper finds it necessary to revise it every two years. Throughout that time, he is continually experimenting and finding new solutions that need to be added.

Marketing the book was his next challenge. Since he hadn't gone through a national publishing company to produce the book, he had to find a way to sell it himself. Thinking his gift of gab might help, he began by talking to bookstore owners personally. He managed to convince several that they could make a profit by selling the books. His friendly personality and his bargaining skills were effective yet again. The book began popping up on shelves in several area bookstores. In addition, he always took a short stack of his books to sit beside him at lectures. People began requesting copies for their friends. And he has kept the cost to a minimum making the book affordable for most people.

Bookstores, realizing that this book could earn them even more profit, requested that Trapper make appearances in the stores to sign the books. It would be advertised on television, his radio programs, and in the newspapers. People came in droves to talk to the man they had heard telling them about easy problem-solvers.

Broadcasting from Minnesota brought a special request. The viewers wanted the solutions to their unique problems written in his book also. People, for instance, wanted to know how to conquer their prairie dog nuisance. They had a huge problem with the cute little rodents that sit straight up beside their dens. Before beginning, Trapper experimented with ways to get rid of prairie dogs, an animal that is similar to the groundhog.

"No one realizes how much alfalfa or how much clover those guys eat. One particular spot a farmer wanted to put him to sleep because the farmer had lost a lot of property. But a farmer can't go up and check his field all the time. He has to wait until a rainy day when he has time.

I told him to find somewhere that they sell kitty litter such as Angels for Animals in Youngstown. You've donated a little money and you'll get used kitty litter. Just take that and put it down the hole around 10 o'clock at night and stomp it down the hole good and tight. Put the whole bag in there. The prairie dog will be out of there in the morning because he cannot handle that used kitty litter and neither can I because of the strong smell of ammonia.

Now how do we know if that prairie dog is coming back? Here's the trick. Put a lot of flour out there around the hole. If he's back, there'll be a footprint in the flour. If the tracks are going back into the hole, I suspect that the farmer didn't put the whole bag in the hole."

The word began spreading across the entire United States like wild fires that Trapper wrote a book. People sent copies to relatives and friends. The Farm and Dairy paper and the Farm Show paper advertised it for him. He couldn't keep up with the demand and eventually a copy of his book could be found in every state.

CHAPTER TWENTY-ONE

THE PRICE OF FAME

Trapper's fame spread more quickly than he had ever anticipated. He had to begin spending more and more time away from his and Elsie's home. He soon realized that he was missing out on the little day-to-day events in his family's life and he really didn't like it. He was torn between giving up this new career that he absolutely loved and staying home with his family that he loved even more.

His fame intruded on his personal life any time he was away from their farm. It became impossible for him to go to restaurants, to walk along the streets in town, or to go into stores without someone talking to him. Followers asked him for advice on their problems and he always felt compelled to take the time to answer.

Elsie soon resisted going anywhere with him. She no longer wanted to accompany him when it was necessary for him to leave the farm. She didn't resent the time Trapper had to spend with others but she was a quiet person who would rather not have crowds of people around her.

Trapper remembers on many occasions that he and Elsie would go into a restaurant to have a nice dinner away from home. The meal would be served piping hot. They would be in the middle of an interesting conversation between eating morsels of food. Then a fan would approach them to offer their praise or to ask for a problem's resolution. And the couple was very polite. They just wouldn't ask anyone to excuse them until they were finished eating. Their dinner would more often than not become cold by the time they could polish off the last bite.

"People came up to ask a two-minute question. And the first thing we'd know, it would be a half-hour long session. I just don't like to explain anything unless I go all the way with it. I want them to know just exactly what to do when they get home. No guess and by garwsh. I like them to do it the right way."

Finally the price of fame became too costly. Trapper was forced into compromising between his family and his career. He decided that it was time to spend more time at home with his family. He knew it was impossible for him to regain the memories that a family makes together. There was no way to recapture the flavor and sentimentality of a moment even if he were told about it.

Trapper and Elsie liked to watch television in the evening when he wasn't lecturing at a speaking engagement or when he wasn't needed at a radio station. It was difficult for Trapper to spend much time just sitting still but he wanted to be with his wife. They watched TV on their small black and white television while Elsie sewed quilts.

One quilt that Trapper remembers in particular was lavender. "Are you sure that will look right when you're done? I sure never saw a quilt like that before."

"You just wait and see. It will be beautiful."

And Elsie "made it work. It was fantastic."

Little did they know while sitting quietly in their living room together on this enjoyable evening what the future would hold for them. They had no way of knowing that this lavender quilt would be the last one Elsie would ever sew.

CHAPTER TWENTY-TWO

LOSING HIS BEST FRIEND

Elsie became ill with Parkinson's disease, sometimes called shaking palsy. Her hands trembled almost constantly and her speech was becoming affected by the dreaded condition. She became tired easily. She was no longer able to take care of her home as she liked. Minor chores went unnoticed by others but it bothered her. She could see wisps of dust collecting under the table while she sat in her chair. She watched more dust layers build day after day but she didn't want to bother Harold with such a petty annoyance. She knew the dusting would be left undone. Medications helped some but doctors said there was no cure for this dreaded disease. It wouldn't be long before she wouldn't be able to swallow even the smallest morsels of food or the most minute sips of water without choking.

Harold tried to make her life as comfortable as he possibly could. He stayed at home with his wife as much as possible and took care of her the best he knew how. If it were necessary to go out for a little while, he would stop at restaurants to eat before going home. He didn't want his Elsie to become even the tiniest bit remorseful that she could no longer prepare the fabulous meals with which she had pleased her husband for so many years.

Then Elsie's birthday arrived. The grandchildren couldn't wait to go to their grandparent's house to celebrate. They begged their parents relentlessly to please hurry and call them for permission to go visit. It was finally February 1, 1994 and they all wanted to wish Grandma Elsie a great day. Her birthdays were always a happy time and a time for ice cream and cake and presents.

But Harold called them first. He hadn't waited for them to walk the short distance in the woods between their homes. He told them, "I think it would be better if you didn't come over right now. Mother's getting too tired and I think she needs to rest a little while. I'm going to help her get into bed."

Before Harold could hang up the receiver and assist her, Elsie called him to her side, "Harold, I'm dying. Now don't feel too sad. We both know that we all die and I know that I'm dying right now. Please. Let's talk a little while before I go."

And they did. They held each other lovingly and said their final goodbyes. They talked for a short time, too short for Harold, before she passed away while sitting in her favorite chair.

Karen heard the telephone ringing. When she picked up the receiver to answer, she heard Harold's shaky voice say, "Mother's gone. What am I gonna' do without her?"

Karen wondered what Harold would do without her, too. He depended on Elsie to be there whenever he came home. He always felt fulfilled when she was by his side in church or whenever they went anywhere together. The thought of living a life without his beloved Elsie was never allowed to cross his mind even for a second.

Once again, Trapper had outlived his spouse. Once again, he was alone and lonely in the world without a mate. Once again, he had to begin his life over without the one he loved.

A few days after the funeral, Harold brought all the children together. He asked everyone to sit around him with himself sitting at the head of the circle. "Now I don't want no hard feelings. I want all of you to take something you want from Elsie's things. But I don't want you to take something and give it to somebody else. I want Elsie's things to stay in our family."

Harold believes that the children honored his request. There was never an argument over her possessions. No one fought over the quilts she so carefully sewed or her recipe books containing all her favorite recipes or any other earthly possessions that Elsie had accumulated in her life. And as far as Harold knows, all of Elsie's special treasures are still being kept within their family today.

He stood up after her collections were divided and said, "Now, let's put this behind us."

And that's how Trapper lives his life. When a family tragedy ends, he closes the door tightly on anything that causes him misery and tries not to look at it ever again. He allows the next new broom to sweep his life clean. He begins focusing on living in the present and enjoying life.

CHAPTER TWENTY-THREE

HIS FINAL LOVE?

Trapper strolled into the Canfield Post Office to empty his ever-full mailbox. Carrying an armload of envelopes, he returned to the parking lot after giving a postal worker a friendly "Good morning". His day had begun without incident and more-than-likely, it would continue in this quiet, run-of-the-mill manner. He had nothing of significant importance planned for the day and he intended to slowly cruise through it instead of tackling the day with his usual haste. But as often happens, an unplanned incident intruded into his life.

A woman walked over to him and without warning gave him a warm hug. "You have a wonderful show. You're such a beautiful person," said Marie.

Taken aback, Trapper thought, 'Here I am in the middle of the parking lot and I'm being hugged by a lovely woman. And I don't even know who she is.' He succumbed to an odd emotion for him. Tears sprang to his eyes. 'Someone cares that much about me. Someone who has never met me before.' He thanked her and she turned and walked away.

His curiosity was peaked. He watched her as she walked down the sidewalk. She looked as if she were gliding on a cloud as she put one foot lightly in front of the other. He continued watching her, as she turned into an enormous apartment complex. He wanted to run after her and talk to her but he knew he would never find the building into which she had gone. It would be like looking for a needle in a haystack.

He suddenly knew he would stop at nothing to find her. Going back inside the post office, he tried to convince the postal employee to give him what he wanted, "You know that young lady that just came in here to get her mail? Can you give me her name and telephone number?"

"Oh no, Trapper. We can't do that," said the woman who was working behind the window.

Realizing he was making no headway, he could feel the tightening of his jaw muscles. He was becoming desperate so he quickly tried another angle, "Let me tell you this. I probably put $10,000 in stamps through this post office. I probably made your payroll. I more-than-likely made your check for the year."

"I'm sorry. I'd lose my job if I gave you any information."

"Oh. OK then," he said dejectedly and he walked out. He didn't know how he would find the stranger now.

He wondered if he visited the post office the same time tomorrow and the next day and the day after that if she would happen to come again. He was just a few feet from the building when he heard a rapping on the window.

"Hey, Trapper, you forgot some mail."

Trapper was positive that he had emptied his mailbox but he went back inside anyway. He unlocked the door and looked in. Lying flat in the box was a small piece of paper. Puzzled, he wondered why he hadn't seen it before. It must have been stuck towards the rear of the box. Then he looked closer. Marie Dornshuld's name and telephone number were neatly written on it. He stuck the paper in his pocket for later.

Trapper finished his work for the day but he had difficulty concentrating. His mind kept wandering back to the sweet woman in the parking lot. He kept feeling her arms around his neck and how great her innocent hug had felt. He wasn't sure what he should do with the piece of paper that was burning a hole in his pocket. He decided to throw caution to the wind and he called her that evening, "Would you like to go to Cortland, Ohio tonight? I have some business I have to do but it won't take me very long."

"I'm sorry I just can't. I promised to be with my sister. We're twins and I couldn't disappoint her."

"Well," he said, "I guess I can postpone this if you'd consider going another day. I was just going to be delivering some of my books anyway."

Trapper and Marie's conversation continued for over an hour. They laughed over the fact that she usually doesn't hug just any strange man but she is a 'hugging person.' He also discovered that Marie Dornshuld had never been to Cortland or to Mosquito Lake. She had never had much opportunity to travel in her married life though she did go to Germany once when her husband was active in the armed forces. She finally agreed to go with Trapper if he could wait until the following day.

That single thirty-five mile drive to Cortland, Ohio proved to be another milestone in both of their lives. The spark of love that they both felt with that one quick embrace in the post office parking lot began growing into a full raging fire. The pair have been together ever since.

Marie doesn't know why she decided to go on a date with Trapper. "I really don't know because I thought I'd always be alone for the rest of my life. And just not go anywhere with any person. I didn't think I'd be with anyone besides my husband. My husband died on January 17, 1988 and then I came to Canfield to live."

Trapper adds with Marie nodding in agreement, "So far, we are very compatible. We agree with most everything and we dance a lot. We follow Joe Fedorchak and we like his music, polkas.

And we like to eat. She'll make a good meal but I'll polish it off because I told her I didn't want her to get pleasingly plump.

I don't know why we met but I think the good Lord made it that way. We go to church every Sunday. And even when we're traveling, if we don't find a church, we watch it on TV.

And another thing, we're both Protestant and I think that worked out fantastic. I joined her church, the Canfield United Methodist Church. I don't participate in the church things very often but that's because we have places to go and things to do. You know I have many lectures to give and shows to do.

But I'll guarantee one thing, I've never missed a church meal yet."

When someone sees the two of them looking at each other, anyone can see that there's a twinkle in their eyes and a smile on their faces. It's obvious that they were destined to be together and that they have a deep respect and love for each other.

"But we do have differences. You can't go through life without differences. But I always say, come on. Let's sit down at the table and have a board meeting. That's when we thrash things out.

Companionship is great! Being alone is bad. Always be with a crowd. Try to find someone you love."

CHAPTER TWENTY-FOUR

RETIREMENT ISN'T IN HIS VOCABULARY

Life with Trapper is one filled with lots of traveling. "It's nothing for us to put 25,000 miles a year on a car. In two years, I always have to buy a new car because there's always over 50,000 miles on it, that's how much traveling we do."

He continued, "It's nothing for me to go 100-200 miles to a big speech. If Marie and I get too tired, we like to layover in a motel some place.

For instance, I'm going to be on Man radio station in Mansfield, Ohio. That's well over 100 miles. Now I don't go on the radio until 10:00. Ordinarily you can make that trip in 2 hours and I go 65-66 mile an hour depending on what the sign tells you. Therefore, we will leave at 6:00 in the morning.

We check in with the radio and tell them we're going down to our favorite spot. We get 'gassed up' on McDonald's coffee and a sandwich before I get on that radio for an hour or an hour and a half.

I like to cut an onion in half and keep it in our car.

Or if we're in a huge crowd, I'll cut an onion in two and put it on the floor beside us. All the bad germs you took in that day will go into that onion and you'll never catch a cold and you'll never catch pneumonia. Just throw that onion away the second day.

One day, Bill Kennedy hired Marie and I to go to Pittsburgh to represent Udder Cream at an American Association of Retired Persons event. Five thousand people came through the door that day. We had the nicest time and we met the nicest people. I was so tired.

We've been to Las Vegas and Minnesota and we enjoy it. We go lots of times for speeches but some times Marie and I have just a fun day."

The couple has traveled to Germany following Joe Fedorchak and his polka band. They thought they took the time to make it entirely a vacation.

When Harold and Marie stepped off the airplane, a television crew rushed up to greet them. Evidently someone had forewarned the German television station about Trapper's reputation in America. They provided a German interpreter for him and interviewed him for a few minutes.

Trapper looked at his watch after the interview was completed and it was 11:45 a.m. German time. He grabbed Marie's hand and hurried her into the airport to find a television set. He wanted to watch his performance and to see if he had done a nice piece of work. To his surprise, they had translated the entire interview into German. His lips were moving but he couldn't understand a single word he had said. They had rushed for nothing.

"But I did enjoy that country and one of the things I enjoyed about it was the coffee. McDonald's coffee of course. That's the only place I know where they sell wine and beer in a McDonald's. But an itty-bitty cup of coffee cost $2.50. It even costs $2.50 for sitting at a table if you only stopped to rest there."

Another oddity seen by Trapper and Marie were pigeons roosting in trees. They were so plentiful that the country had begun giving the birds a form of birth control to help curb their population. Supposedly, if a person is walking down the street and he/she manages to dodge getting rained on with bird droppings, it's a sign of good luck.

After Germany, Harold and Marie went to Slovenia. "I'd never thought I'd see a country that didn't have silos. You see, they grow corn but they don't have any silos. They're doing things the old fashioned way," says Harold. Another vacation for them was to Frankenmuth, Michigan. They attended a polka dance there also. There were five polka bands playing at the same time with 10,000 square feet of dance floor in front of them. To his utter amazement, someone announced that Harold Bailey, the Friendly Trapper, was there from Ohio and to feel free to ask him any questions. Well, there went the dancing because people recognized the white floppy hat with the blue band that now has several favorite pins fixed onto the front.

He was easy to spot right away. Trapper and Marie would lose a dance or two while he explained something.

Joe Fedorchak frequents a town and resort called Seven Springs in Southwest Pennsylvania. Harold and Marie always plan to attend his performance. Joe never fails to announce that the Friendly Trapper is in the building. He tells people, "Go ask him about your crickets." There goes the dance. But Harold never minds because he always participates in the one thing he thrives upon, helping people.

Retiring is definitely not in Trapper's vocabulary. At 73, he's still going strong. He has more energy than most people half his age. And thanks to Marie, he's one hundred percent organized. He relies solely on her to keep a calendar of events for them. Every morning when they arise, they first head to that calendar. In a one-inch square space, there may be as many as three speeches printed for the day. If they're lucky, they may only have to travel 50 miles. And when the day is over but before they can think about retiring for the night, they once again head to the calendar.

Together, they're heading through life laughing and loving and savoring every single minute. Will they ever stop the mad rush from town to town? Will they ever be able to lay their heads upon their pillows without worrying where they have to go the next day? Somehow, slowing down doesn't seem to fit in a life with the Friendly Trapper. Because Trapper and Marie never know when the next new broom will be sweeping their lives clean.

"We are substantially different people capable of substantially different things at the various stages of our lives. Our attitudes, philosophies, talents, and enthusiasms go through surprising transformations and once gone, can rarely be revisited....At every stage of your creative life, drain the cup dry...These are unique moments in your life for turning out pages or performances that you may not feel motivated to produce, or able to produce, five or ten years from now."

–Robert Orben

ABOUT THE AUTHOR

Wendy Drescher began life in Leavittsburg, Ohio where she continues to reside, a mere six blocks from where both she and her father grew up.

She is a recognized speaker who enjoys impersonating Elizabeth Cady Stanton and Harriet Taylor Upton, famous American suffragettes because there's a bit of a rebel deep inside her conservative exterior. She is known for transforming into Sally Klingensmith, a purely fictional character while sporting pink high-top tennis shoes and straw hat. She also educates others about Grave's Disease, a condition that ended her school-nursing career. Regardless of the subject, Wendy is sure to include plenty of laughs in her presentations.

Wendy graduated from St. Luke's Hospital School of Nursing in Cleveland, Ohio and earned her degree from St. Joseph's College in Maine. Wendy is published in "The People of Trumbull County", the Northeast Ohio Education Association Journal, the National Grave's Disease Foundation publication, and numerous nursing papers and newsletters.

TO ORDER ADDITIONAL COPIES OF "EVERY NEW BROOM SWEEPS CLEAN":

INCLUDE:

NAME_____

ADDRESS_____

CITY_____**STATE**____**ZIP**____

TELEPHONE__(___)_____

COST PER BOOK	$15.00
TAX PER BOOK	1.00
SHIPPING/HANDLING	5.00
TOTAL COST PER BOOK	**$21.00**

QUANTITY WANTED_____at **$21.00/book**

MONEY INCLUDED $_____